Dear Ru...

What ... you're to have such a kind, friendly & caring guest like you here for 8 days!

Fed Up ... to Wonderstruck

We have enjoyed your company a lot & hope to see you again! And we still have the weekend ☺, hope to get to hang ~~out~~ with you more. ♡Kristina

Fed Up ...
to Wonderstruck

What

happened

when I

no longer

trusted

anything

but the

unknown

Kristina Kashyap

Published by:

Kristina Kashyap

Edition 1.1

Copyright © 2019 Kristina Kashyap

ISBN 978-0-578-54045-0

Editor: Dinah Steward

Cover Photo: Vivek Kashyap

Author Photo: Aryadne Woodbridge

Interior and Cover Design: Neil S. White

Printed in the United States of America

Updates + New Chapters in Life:

www.feduptowonderstruck.com

TO

THE

ONE

&

all those

who want to experience more

wonder

and connection as

they traverse

the universe

Broken Open Heart

No matter how shattered or shutdown it's been

Despite not knowing where to begin

Find the crevice where the light breaks through

The place where hope's flicker is holding true

And fan that flame with determination

A broken heart can lead to liberation

Do not believe simply what your eyes reveal

There are so many secrets they cannot steal

An innocent heart is like an alchemist stone

For the universe to begin to unfold-all untold

An open heart is a key

To unlock fantastic mysteries

Contents

Preface — *xiii*

Acknowledgments — *xvii*

Part I

Chapter 1
The Journey Begins — 3

Chapter 2
Costa Rica — 17

Chapter 3
Coming Home — 27

Chapter 4
Into the Depths, I Go — 37

Chapter 5
Healing in the Subtle Realm — 49

Chapter 6
The Death of Death — 57

Part II

Chapter 7
Magical to Practical — 69

Chapter 8
Creating a Relationship of Trust with #1

  1 A Lasting Relationship — 77
  2 Essential Silence Time — 79
  3 Follow Your Heart — 81
  4 Trust Your Intuition — 85
  5 Cheer Yourself On — 88

Chapter 9

Creating a Relationship of Trust with God

    1 Open To Possibility   91

    2 Speak Your Truth   93

    3 Better Listen Up   94

    4 Experiment & Explore   99

    5 Relax & Enjoy   101

Chapter 10

Creating Relationships of Trust with Others

    1 Not About You   103

    2 Benefit Of Doubt   106

    3 Give Others Time   108

    4 In Your Lane   109

    5 Healing With Others   111

Chapter 11

Creating a Relationship of Trust with Matter

    1 Appreciating Your Vehicle   115

    2 Listening For Signals   118

    3 Big Game Changer   120

    4 Consumer To Contributor   123

    5 Our Choices Matter   125

Chapter 12

Creating a Relationship of Trust with Life

    1 Be Here Now   129

    2 Cycle Of Generosity   131

    3 Light = Right = Might   134

    4 Find Your Practices   136

    5 All Together Now   139

Conclusion   *141*

Every Ending is another Beginning   *143*

About the Author   *147*

Preface

I love this quote from Buddha:

Do not believe in anything simply because you have heard it.
Do not believe in anything simply because
it is spoken and rumored by many.
Do not believe in anything simply because
it is found written in your religious books.
Do not believe in anything merely on
the authority of your teachers and elders.
Do not believe in traditions because they
have been handed down for many generations.
But after observation and analysis, when you find that anything
agrees with reason and is conducive to the good and benefit
of one and all, then accept it and live up to it.

- Buddha

... and as for me, I would add: accept it only after you have experienced it for yourself. At least that has been my method of understanding myself and the world around me. Life has been my laboratory. I have done some fascinating experiments and feel I have gotten some interesting results. As any good scientist would,

I have always needed the results to prove themselves several times over before I can accept them. What I know to be true has been hard-won.

This book chronicles my quest to find meaning and myself. What began as a desperate attempt to climb out of the confusion brought on by trauma in my life ultimately led me to understand how much joy, bliss, and freedom are available to every one of us right now. I just had to learn to be open and ask the right questions.

I have cherry-picked the most unforgettable moments on my journey to a broader understanding and revitalized trust in life. I invite you to come with me on this odyssey of the heart, as some universal truths unveil themselves and I marvel at the absolute wonder of it all.

You will see, though, that my pathway to trusting in life again was no ordinary undertaking. I wasn't willing to believe just anything to satisfy my need for consolation. I had to become open to the possibility that I may or may not like the answers I discovered. What was most important to me was that my existential experiments be completely unbiased.

Every person's journey winds differently through space and time. What you will find here is not a route that is just like yours, nor one that you need to emulate. But, perhaps in journeying with me through these experiences, you will find a connection with your own adventures of heart and soul. Something you read here may open up a new way of seeing a particular aspect of your life, allowing more curiosity and wonder to flow in – much like what happened to me.

Although it is not easy to put these experiences into words, I will try to express them tangibly so that you may be able to feel the wonder of them - even now - just as I did at that time. The only guideline for myself in sharing these personal experiences is to be honest and real, so that you can witness unfiltered how I went from a complete lack of trust to total trust.

I think my experiences highlight many profound questions, and the answers that I found were true for me. Two that are especially close to my heart are: How do we begin to rebuild trust in life when we feel life has completely broken our trust? Is possible to feel that we are eternally safe and supported in the universe again?

A wise person once told me, "When everyone in the world is operating out of trust, that will be heaven." That person was my husband, Vivek Kashyap. I immediately understood the truth of that statement. Because, when we operate from a place of deep trust, we will experience more openness, freedom, love, belonging, and connection. What a beautiful world that will be!

Acknowledgments

First, I would like to thank my husband, Vivek Kashyap, for his precious and tireless support throughout the writing of this book. Your faith and encouragement increased my courage and enthusiasm for the journey, each step of the way!

Unlimited thanks from the bottom of my heart to my fantastic friend and editor, Dinah Steward. This process was greatly enriched because of your magic touch and close attention to detail!

Also, thank you to my marvelous friends that have given me their tremendous support and valuable feedback as I wrote this book: Yolanda, Michelle, Pratibha, Colleen, Aarti, Marcela, Ione, Pat, Sneha, Punam, Lorien, Vinoo, Sister Gita, Grace, Nancy, Warren, Candice, Guilda, Liza, Tara, Karen, Kevin, Mina, Geetika, Sukh, Uma, Monika, Nadira, Sonya, Suzanne, Newsha, Vaibhav, Dennis, Dad, Angie, Loraine, & Bebe's parents.

Additionally, love and gratitude to all my friends and family, who may be unnamed here but have made an immense difference in this process and my life. We don't do anything as an island. Thank you for your love, encouragement, care, support, cooperation, and good wishes. Together we can accomplish anything.

Part I

Cause

1

The Journey Begins

What am I supposed to think
When I'm on the brink
What am I supposed to do
When I'm without you

There I was on the beach, sitting *under* the towel which I had brought to sit *on*. There was a steady stream of tears running down my cheeks. Passersby may have wondered why I was under the towel, or if I was OK.

I wasn't.

What would I say if they asked me what was wrong? I didn't know exactly where I was, internally. Perhaps this was rock bottom? It seemed hard enough. I was feeling perplexed and helpless. I didn't know who or what to trust anymore. But, at least nature was still a respite and a place I could land.

The decade leading up to this moment had been a roller coaster ride from hell, the kind that gives you whiplash. Fortunately, life was relatively normal before the double-digit years. As a child, I was outgoing and affectionate. You could find me entertaining and cuddling everyone. During bleaker times, my mom would ask me, "Kristina, how are you always so happy?" That innate happiness, which I had been born with, stayed with me up until the biggest challenge of my life, which landed me under the towel on the beach.

Before the age of ten, my mom, dad, sister, and I lived together. We had a pony named Streak, a dog named Blackie, and a cat named Peaches. We lived close enough to my paternal grandparents to see them at least once a week. Sundays were the best! They meant grandma's three-course Italian dinner with the extended family. Everyone would gather around the table, eager to see what was on the menu that day. Was it any of our favorites? There was always plenty of laughter and extra helpings just a few steps away if they weren't already on the brimming table. My grandma loved to feed people and was an expert at making the food so good ... that you wished you had two stomachs to fill.

Our early dinner would finish around two o'clock, and the rest of the day was spent enjoying each other's company, in each one's preferred way. Some would stay at the table and play rummy. Others would go to the living room to watch a game. Sometimes we went down to the basement to listen to music or played outside at the nearby park. The options seemed endless. It was Sunday after all!

I particularly loved playing rummy with my grandpa, the card-shark, who would try to find a way to lose so

I could win. My first significant loss and introduction to death were at age ten when he passed away suddenly. I will never forget my mom coming to pick me up at school midday. She looked very sad, so I asked, "What's wrong mom?" She knelt down in the empty school hallway, hugged me, and told me that my grandpa had passed away. Up until then, I thought that he would live forever. I had never considered that anything could happen to him or anyone I loved. I was stupefied at his casket, holding his cold hand and sobbing, I didn't want ever to let go of him. My dad had to come to peel me away so that others could pay their respects.

From there, everything seemed to go downhill, with some very steep drops along the way. Some of the steepest were the divorce of my parents; moving from the Midwest to Florida without my father and sister; my mother's alcoholism; her brain injury at the hands of her wealthy fiancé; a college sexual assault; and the loss of my hero to suicide.

In those years, I lost my mom not once – but three times. First to alcoholism, then to domestic violence, and finally to her death just before my seventeenth birthday. In each instance, I tried to save her ... if I could just love her enough, maybe she would get healthy again. I remembered the times when she was present, playful, kind, and friendly with literally everyone. At that time, she was an involved parent who did things like lead the Girl Scouts and have special birthday parties for us. That was all before she got hijacked by an ever-increasing need for constant wine and beer.

I idolized my mom when I was little and imagined her to be the best mom in the world. I genuinely thought that I could help bring her back to me, my sister, and her old self. But that never materialized. Her life ended after a domestic abuse incident, which caused brain damage and left her in an incapacitated state. My maternal grandfather and I became a team; he would pick me up after school and drive me to see her. Both my grandfathers have been such tenderhearted figures in my life. We took care of my mom together, making sure she had her diapers changed and was being fed and bathed properly. I tried to help her in any way I could. I was desperate for her to survive.

Since I was a baby, though, I had always had another place where I could be mothered when I needed it. My Aunt Roseanne, who was my Godmother, was like my second mom. She had been a touchstone of superhero proportions in my life. Whenever my sister and I would go to visit her, she was always doing things with us that were fun and nurturing, like making cookies and cakes or taking us to parks and museums. After she moved to Michigan, we didn't see her as often but would still get care packages in the mail. They would have her famous chocolate chip banana bread, a beautiful card, and other fun things she picked up along the way as she thought of us.

Besides knowing how to make people feel incredibly loved, she was a woman of significant accomplishments (having earned two PhDs by the time she was 27); she was an active philanthropist and a champion for people subjected to any form of discrimination. She worked especially hard on behalf of women, African Americans, Native Americans, and domestic abuse victims. She represented the best of human beings to me, and what it looked like to have a big, compassionate heart.

She was the most cultured, educated, and well-traveled person in my family. She instilled in me a love for learning about new places and people. For example, within a year of my high school graduation, she took me to Jamaica to meet some of her academic friends. She also sent me to Honduras to help build houses with Habitat for Humanity. These were just some of the ways she helped expose me to new people and places, which taught me that I was a part of a global family.

During my first year of college, while I was still struggling to come to terms with my mother's death, she was a rock for me. I even went to live with her for a few months, after my first semester, when I was going through a particularly rough patch. But, in my second year of college, *inconceivably*, she committed suicide. No one in our family even knew that she was depressed. She always put on a smile and prioritized being there for everyone else, but apparently, she was struggling inside. Oh, how I wished, more than anything, I had known. I would have done anything to try and help her!

She was my hero and my role model. I was shattered. Up until then, she had been the one with whom I had always identified the most in my life; we had so many similar characteristics, interests, and mannerisms. My dad used to mistakenly call me by her name because I reminded him of her so much. (See photo of us at the end of the book.)

One of the most difficult experiences in life is when your mother passes, and it is even more intolerable when it seems tragically avoidable. I lost both of my mother figures in such a short period, and perhaps when I needed them the most. It was as if the anchors had been severed from the ship of my life, and I began drifting this way and that way without control or safety. Don't get me wrong – I love my dad and he has been a true rock for me. He has taught me so much of what I know, by living a principled life and having a big heart. But my sister was a daddy's girl, and I was a momma's girl. At that time, for me, Mother = Life.

I was also grappling with the fact that I had learned, post-injury for my mom and postmortem for my aunt, that they were both sexually abused when they were young. Neither of them was able to process and heal those traumatic experiences within themselves, and this had devastating effects.

Having been through those losses left me not just wanting for normalcy, but also not knowing what "normal" was anymore. Hence, me: under the towel, sitting on the sand, face in my hands. I had lost all sense of solid ground under my feet. My trust in life was shredded. All the while, my contemporaries were living *their* lives in the customarily expected order, with the usual milestones: high school, college, relationships, engagement, marriage, babies ... and so on and so forth.

Despite everything I had gone through in high

school, I was somehow able to keep myself together enough to gain a full scholarship to college. As a young person, I should have been energized and thrilled to study and learn. Why wasn't I? I had many interests and hobbies growing up, such as singing, dancing, acting, and later, holistic medicine. However, all of that seemed suddenly pointless. I couldn't understand how I could move forward in life when I didn't know what the purpose of it all was. I knew that happiness and fulfillment are what everyone wants. But, based on what I had observed in my life, I also knew that lasting happiness could not be found in money, career, education, appearance, relationships, or accomplishments. True happiness had to come from somewhere deep and unchangeable; that is, if it was going to be worth pursuing.

In seeking my true, lasting happiness, I felt a desire to understand if God was real or merely a figment of people's hope. I had been taught about God from early childhood and felt a sense of connection with God through my late teens, but after everything that had happened, I wasn't sure if God existed. Certain things that I was taught didn't make sense anymore, i.e., the idea that God was pulling all the strings, deciding when and how we are born, and when we die. If God existed, why was there so much suffering? Why would there be longer lives for some, but shorter for others? Why would some children be subjected to abuse and neglect? My experiences of pain became the filter through which I examined everything; I didn't feel connected to God at that time. I only felt sorrow. At some point, grief has a way of displacing faith.

I had friends and family who were active in different religions, as well as various denominations of Christianity, including Catholicism. There were also people in my life who didn't believe in God anymore. I didn't know anyone who could guide me without the personal bias of their own belief or disbelief. My inner compass had broken, my faith in people was shaken, and I didn't know if there was any Divine Source to guide me. Yet, I desperately needed direction. From my vantage point, that left just one option: To trust the great unknown and see if, by some chance, I might be guided by something.

On the beach, under the towel, when the tears stopped flowing, a little mantra emerged from my heart: "Whatever you are, if you are, show me the way." To whom or what was I calling out? I didn't know. Was there anyone or anything on the receiving end? No idea. But I did know one thing: If I was going to decide which direction to go in life, I had first to understand who I was and why I was here. I needed to understand life's purpose and my place in it.

Something shifted within me as I began to recite my heart's mantra. I felt a sense of curiosity, side-by-side with my uncertainty and doubt; but at least there was an opening which started to let the pressure of confusion out. I didn't know what to expect in terms of a response, so I decided not to expect anything at all! I was good at that by now: expecting the worst, so I could delay the disappointment and unsafety that might follow.

There I was, heart in my hands, handing it to the universe or whatever might hear me, hoping that it would be able to provide some direction in this progressively confusing experience called life. That first week, a couple of things happened. Someone recommended a book to me that they were reading: *Autobiography of a Yogi* by Paramahansa Yogananda. I didn't go to buy it because I didn't want to be influenced by anything external. So I stayed with my heart's mantra: "Whatever you are, if you are, show me the way."

A few days later, another person recommended the same book to me. What were the odds? I took the hint and made my way to the bookstore, at first chance. I remember seeing the cover for the first time, with the portrait of an interesting-looking spiritual man with long hair and piercing eyes. I saw that it had been published long ago, which made having it recommended by two people, just days apart, very mysterious. I started to read the thick book, taking my time to take it in. I remember being intrigued by the author's experiences because they were beyond what I thought was possible. There was something about the way he shared that seemed honest and heartfelt. It was an exercise in trust to read it with an open mind, but the uncanny way the book found its way to me made it easier to give it a chance.

That same week, I was invited to attend a nada yoga workshop (an Indian system of inner transformation through sound and tone), in which we were chanting and singing for most of the day. In the last half hour, we were invited to get up and dance. I was surprised that, as I moved, it felt as if I was *being* moved. I was going along with the flow, as the energy and music seemed to move my body effortlessly.

After the workshop, I went to visit my friend Neil, who was nearing the end of ten days of silence he was taking for himself. He was someone with whom I could have deep and meaningful conversations on any topic. Although he was philosophical, he was also scientific; needing to see things in order to believe them (just like me). When I got to his place, he was busy working on something. I decided to do some sun salutations (a series of yoga poses performed in a continuous flow) as I waited for him, to counteract a day of mostly sitting. As I moved through the sun salutations, I was experiencing a level of strength that I had never experienced before. I wondered what I had tapped into, to feel so much stronger than usual.

When Neil and I sat down to chitchat, arranged on opposite ends of the couch, I began describing my day to him. As we were talking, I suddenly couldn't see him anymore; but I could still hear his voice. I said, "I can't see you!" And he said, "I can't see you either!" He then slowly started to re-appear to me in the form of light, from the top down. I repeatedly blinked my eyes, trying to see if it was something faulty with my vision. But no amount of blinking changed what I was seeing. I first saw his fluffy hair, then his face and lastly the entire shape of his body – all in light. As this was happening, I was describing it to him, and he told me that he was seeing the same thing happen to me.

We were simultaneously experiencing a truly unusual phenomenon, which left us speechless and mesmerized. It was a very transformative experience, as we were both seeking answers to the bigger questions at that time.

The combination of amazing experiences that I had that day made it clear that I was starting to get a response from my heart's mantra: "Whatever you are, if you are, show me the way." This increased the fire of my curiosity even more. I began to look forward to what might happen next.

Before my little beach meltdown, my childhood best friend Candice and I had solidified plans to live together. We were each at a crossroads in our lives and were trying to figure out what was next. She had packed up her life in Ohio, to move where I was living in Florida, and she would be arriving the next day. She didn't know about my heart's call to the universe; nobody did for that matter. This quest was between my truth and me. When Candice arrived, I had just had those surprising experiences the day before. Because of this, my heart and mind were pulled even more towards my inner search. This mantra became like a heartbeat, constantly and automatically repeating within.

Candice and I began talking about the possibility of traveling to Costa Rica together before finding a permanent place. As we were in the process of deciding, I had another unprecedented experience: complete silence of the mind. It became still, without any extra thoughts. During those extraordinary few days, I was having only necessary and precise thoughts. There was nothing wasteful. My mind seemed to be there only to receive cues from my inner knowing, which felt like it had been turned up to levels I had never felt before. For three days, I knew just what to do, when to do it and how to do it — without needing to think about it. This same experience repeated three times over the next few months.

Each time it happened, it felt like I had tapped into an effortless way of being. After a couple of days with my mind that free, my face would begin to shine, and people would start to notice. My yoga teacher asked me, "What are you doing differently?" I was simply focusing on the mantra in my heart, and the inner environment of my mind became completely clear. All direction was coming from an inner knowing and not from my mind. During those days, I had no questions, confusion, or worries. I was experiencing a present and liberated state in which I didn't have to think at all; the results of which were noticeable in my body, my energy, and the accuracy of my thoughts and actions.

After the first of these experiences, I was trying to stay on the same page with Candice about living and traveling together. It was becoming clear, however, that I was getting more of a response to my heart's longing and each experience increased my desire to follow the wormhole further. "Whatever you are, if you are, show me the way," was now a two-way communication. What was I being shown? Was the last experience of having a clear and silent mind, where I easily followed my inner knowing, showing me a path or goal of some kind? I did not understand what this communication meant; I just knew I was receiving it. And I was elated.

I realized that I needed to be completely tuned into what was happening in my inner world. Because of the strong pull of introversion and introspection, I didn't want to engage in the "normal" things that other 22-year-old girls wanted to do. I didn't want to explore new places, go dancing, or even go to the beach; I just needed to find answers to the bigger questions. I knew that if I went to Costa Rica with Candice, it would be hard for me not to do those fun things. She has a way of pulling out of me the more adventurous aspects of my personality (which I normally love). But I felt strongly that I needed to go somewhere, alone ... not away from her, but away from everyone I knew. It was as if I was being called to renounce everything except my quest.

I heeded the call to seek the truth, without the influence of anyone I knew, relationship patterns I'd developed, or societal pressures. Once it was clear that I needed this time to be with myself, I communicated that to Candice. Being the understanding person she is, she loved and cared for me through it all. It wasn't easy to tell her (nor, I'm sure, was it easy for her to hear it), but I felt an overwhelming push from within to honor what I needed to do and to trust whatever was going to happen. I didn't know what was next – yet. But, because I started to get subtle responses, I knew it was going to be good!

2

Costa Rica

Hearts longing shot out like an arrow
Who was hearing this song sparrow
What's next on the journey, can't know
Which direction will the path now show

I found an organic farm in Costa Rica, where I could live and work while I was there. It looked like it would be an ideal spot to be with me, my new book, and my journal. I also thought doing some gardening might be a meditative way to connect with nature.

Getting to the farm was an adventure. It wasn't my first time in Central America, but it was my first time arriving by plane – followed by a bus and then a speedboat taxi to get to my destination. The farm was beautiful, bordered by the beach and tropical ocean. However, after a few days of being there, I realized that they weren't doing much farming; it was more like a party farm and not the peaceful place I was envisioning. The environment was made significantly worse by the pushy young owner of the farm, who didn't seem to be able to take no for an answer. He came on to me and my bunkmate, Michaelanne, so many times that we eventually left the farm together to find better accommodations in the nearest town.

After a long trek through the rainforest, we found ourselves a quaint little place that we could share. It was a significant upgrade from the party farm! My roommate wanted to go to the beach all day, which left ample space for me to read, journal, contemplate, and try my hand at meditation. I would sit to meditate with my eyes closed, legs crossed in the lotus position, and hold my mantra as my intention. Sometimes my body would vibrate from side to side, and when it stopped, my body and mind would become very still. I also started to see tiny points of light while my eyes were closed. I didn't know what either of those phenomena meant, but they seemed to be further communication coming from outside of myself. My heart's mantra was now turning into a conversation, even though I didn't know yet who or what was on the other end.

From time to time, I would make my way to an internet café to email my dad, assuring him that I was fine. One day, I saw a poster on the wall of that café, which read, "Meditate on the Beach." It was advertising a Raja Yoga meditation class that would be held just a mile from where I was staying. I felt a very strong pull to go. It was ten days out. I marked the calendar and was counting down the days with excitement.

When the day finally arrived, I joined my fellow

hopeful meditators for the class at a house across from the beach. Michaelanne and one of her new friends decided to join me. The host asked everyone to come up on the deck and face the ocean. Two teachers had traveled from 4 hours away to give a 2-hour class. They talked about the intrinsic qualities of the self, being: peace, love, purity, power, wisdom, and bliss. They also explained that we are eternal beings – souls – and *not* the body. In the last part of the class, they led an open-eyed meditation with a guided commentary about the soul.

During the guided meditation, I had my first experience of myself as consciousness beyond the body. I felt weightless, free from the body, and yet aware of the body at the same time. It was as if my body was a dress or a costume, but it wasn't me. I understood that I was the one seeing through my eyes. It was clear to me that I was not the physical body, but the distinct consciousness within it. During the meditation, I saw many tiny points of light again; only this time, my eyes were open. I understood now what I was possibly seeing – since during the class – the teachers explained that the soul is an incorporeal, tiny point of light.

The class finished, and the other students started leaving. I wondered if I was the only one having what felt like a supernatural experience. Perhaps it was a natural experience, but I was having it for the first time. Knowing that I was a non-physical being opened up a greater possibility for me that God might exist. I had to find out what else these teachers knew.

I rushed up to them with enthusiasm, to start the great inquiry. I told them about my experience in meditation and asked them, "Does God exist? And, if so, why is there so much sorrow in the world?"

They kindly invited me to sit with them at a table in the backyard as they shared their understanding of God. They said God is a being of peace, love, purity, power, wisdom, and bliss – similar to the soul. However, they pointed out that God is the *Ocean* of these qualities, the infinite source, which we can tap into in meditation, thus reminding ourselves who we truly are. They described many ways to connect with God through various aspects of God's personality and different relationships. They said that God could be experienced as our Mother, Father, Teacher, Guide, Friend, and Beloved. Their description of God was unlike anything I had previously heard – and by far the most beautiful. After that powerful first guided meditation, I knew that God's existence was possible. But, I wouldn't know if it was a reality unless I had a direct experience myself. In any case, it was fascinating to talk with them, and their peaceful demeanors were speaking to me in ways that were beyond words.

After getting my biggest questions answered, I asked where I could learn more about this type of meditation. They said that my timing was perfect because the next weekend they were having a retreat which I was welcome to attend. I bought myself a bus ticket for the five-hour ride north. As I traveled on the Costa Rican highway, which wound its way through the lowland rainforest, I began to feel a sense of contentment taking up residence where only the longing for answers had been. It was clear now, on this path of discovery, I had some sort of guide. Trickling in was a new trust which sat firmly next to my curiosity. I couldn't wait to see if anything new would happen over the weekend.

The simple retreat center nestled in the quiet valley town of San Cristobal didn't have much activity, except for the arrival of our energetic retreat group. I entered the property with only my backpack and mantra. But now, it was more like, "Keep showing me the way." Each new experience was like a bread crumb, and I, the earnest bird, was eagerly following the trail.

The senior meditation teacher who had come from the U.S., especially for the retreat, lived extremely close to where I lived in Florida. What were the chances? It felt like these Raja Yoga teachers were being sent to where I was. She opened the retreat with a short talk about the soul, followed by a guided meditation. We were asked to find a point of focus to meditate on. I looked ahead at a poster, which was next to the teacher. During the meditation, I began to see a crown and robe made of light, which was on her head and draped over her shoulders, respectively. I blinked a few times to see if I was mistaken, but they both stayed visible for the duration of the meditation.

Once the class was over and everyone broke for dinner, I found my way to her table. "Can I ask you a question? During the meditation, I saw a crown and robe made of light on your head and shoulders. What does that mean?" She told me that perhaps I saw this in connection with the aim of Raja Yoga meditation because the goal is to become a self-sovereign, a master of the mind and senses. She said the word Raja itself translated as "king."

If I was getting a vision of the *aim* of this kind of meditation, before I knew anything about it, then it seemed like a direct invitation to learn it. I realized that I was correctly following the signals I was receiving ... since they kept coming and were making more sense as I went along.

The weekend program focused on having awareness of one's divine qualities and developing more self-respect. The knowledge they shared with us about the soul felt instinctively on-point and in alignment with what I was experiencing, too. Throughout the weekend, when I would meditate in the retreat sessions, my room, or the gardens outside, I would feel those subtle vibrations move within me and would see the tiny points of light. I didn't feel alone anywhere. I knew that I was in some kind of non-verbal communication with that which was guiding me.

After the retreat, since I was already so close to the meditation center in San Jose, I went directly to take the Raja Yoga meditation course. It was an open space with light pouring through the windows, highlighting the plants and flowers, which gave it an organic feeling. There was a deep serenity and spiritual lightness throughout. On the first day, one of the teachers taught about soul consciousness, the mind, intellect, and sanskaras (memories and ingrained habits). She showed me an image of a tiny, luminous point of light, similar to the points of light I had been seeing for several weeks. The information felt plausible when compared to my own experiences. Our classes opened and closed with beautiful guided meditations.

Many times when we would meditate, I would enter the more subtle space of the soul, which was calm, peaceful, and felt like home. I was reawakening to something deep, real, and eternal within myself. It felt both familiar and wonderfully new. The second day they taught about God and karma. On the last day, they talked about time, and the journey of human consciousness throughout it. I felt invigorated. Every subtle experience in meditation was reaffirming my journey forward, letting me know that I was on the right track. And this knowledge I was absorbing explained the phenomena that I was experiencing. They went hand-in-hand.

Since the meditation center was four hours away from where I was previously staying, I listened to my heart and went down to collect my things. I rented out a guest room that was only 20 minutes from the meditation center. I would practice meditation before going to sleep and after waking up; during which time, I would see the points of light and feel the same vibrations throughout my body. I would leave early for the center to be there for meditation by 6 am. I was dancing and skipping in my mind as I walked. It felt as if I was holding a bunch of balloons that were lifting me into the air. I was being swept off my feet, falling in love with this new world that was opening up.

I was so excited to be in that spiritual environment every day. Now, for the first time, I was around many other people who were spending their time contemplating the deeper spiritual truths. It was the most magical time in my life, discovering myself as an eternal soul!

One evening there was a public program offered at the meditation center. I asked if I could help. I was given the task of opening the door as people entered. I sat in the last row, near the back of the room, so that I could let people in. Once everyone was there, and the meditation had begun, I went into a deep stage of meditation. But this time I saw something new ... the subtle bodies of everyone in front of me were visible. Everyone in the room was lit up. Up until that point, I had seen this only once before, with my friend Neil. But *this* was an entire room! We were immersed in a spiritual layer of reality, which had apparently always been there, but I had not been able to see. I sat mesmerized as I witnessed everyone in the peaceful glow of this subtle region of light.

As the days turned into weeks, I found myself at the meditation center in the morning, during the day, and on the weekends, too. I wanted to understand as much as I could about myself and the spiritual nature of life. These experiences in meditation were knocking down the walls of disbelief and distrust that I had built up. A new multi-layered world was opening up for me. I could hardly contain my thirst for diving deeper into spiritual knowledge. It was a joint venture of the head and the heart.

I began to notice that, when I wanted to understand a new aspect of spirituality, it would naturally come up – often in the next day's class. These were questions and thoughts that I had not discussed with anyone else. This made me feel even more heard, embraced, and supported by the universe.

As my trip was nearing its end, my dad came for a visit. We went down to the beach town I had initially stayed in, and I showed him around. He enjoyed the local Costa Rican food, art, and culture. Then we went to Bocas del Toro, Panama for a short visit. I enjoyed spending time with him, but my attention was way beyond sightseeing!

My internal need was to keep exploring the soul. I wondered if he noticed that I was different. I took him to the meditation center, but I couldn't tell him everything I was experiencing because it seemed like it would be too hard for anyone to believe. For now, it was still *my* secret with the One that was responding to me.

3

Coming Home

You tickled my sense-ability
A sixth sense awakened within me
You showed me the sky
A web of twinkling dancing stars
And told me I belong among them

I went to Costa Rica, not understanding who I was. I came back knowing, without a doubt, that I was a Spiritual Being having a human experience. I felt reconnected to myself and that which was infinite. I was home, but different. My world had expanded into new layers, dimensions, and depths. I felt like a resident of a richer universe. From now on, home would be where I could be my true self and have a genuine sense of belonging. And I could carry that with me wherever I went.

I continued to meditate daily at home and was getting clear thoughts about what I needed to do next, and acting on them without a doubt. The more time

I dedicated to silence and connection, the more I was tapping into my innate guidance system. I was in the process of learning to trust myself and life, too.

Meditation zoomed me out from the microscopic perspective to a more unlimited view, where I could see the perfection of life. It helped me tap into the bigger picture, beyond the limited perceptions I had of myself, others, and time.

How I understood the world, and moved within it, changed dramatically once I knew myself as a spiritual being. I didn't see myself as defined by the characteristics of the body or the experiences of one lifetime anymore. I understood that my existence and eternal story spanned much beyond that. I couldn't be summed up – or sum anyone else up – by worldly standards, because souls are inherently worthy. I didn't see differences based on the gender, race, age, or religion of anyone. I understood that all are eternal divine beings, full of the wealth of divine qualities. I did not know who a soul had been in the past, where they currently were on their inner journey, or what they were going to be in the future. But I did know that all were souls – equally worthy of love, respect, consideration, and care.

Shortly after coming back from Costa Rica, I went to a meditation retreat at Peace Village Learning and Retreat Center in the Catskill Mountains of New York. Being there, meditating with over 150 other people, taught me the power of a gathering. It was effortless to connect within myself in that pure environment. I felt a sense of being home, with the warmheartedness of the people and serenity that permeated the atmosphere. I also took time to connect with nature on their hearty 300 acres of pristine mountain land. It was a weekend of deepening the connection with myself and others on a spiritual path. I felt as if I had been wrapped in a blanket of love.

It was there that I found out that the Brahma Kumaris, the organization with whom I was learning Raja Yoga, had their headquarters in Mt. Abu, India; a place where 25,000 people would meditate together. Having already gained so much from what I was learning, I decided that the next step was to go to the place where it had all begun. I flew to India on the wings of excitement and curiosity. When I stepped off the plane in Delhi, the smell of the air – a mix of earthiness and ash – seemed familiar. It was like I had been there before.

On the rest of the journey to Mt. Abu, I became captivated by India. It was the most colorful, wild, and exciting place I had ever been. It was like being in an interactive circus. There was a vast array of different types of people, clothing, buildings (accommodation and temples), and modes of transportation; there was so much variety in one panorama, and it was all so colorful! Many types of vehicles shared the road: brightly painted trucks, rickshaws, cars, bicycles, scooters, mopeds, people riding camels, oxcarts, and horses. The traffic would stop for cows to cross at their leisure. Nothing could be expected, and yet it all somehow worked.

Once we arrived in Mt. Abu, it was like entering

another world, which was in stark contrast to the colorful chaos I saw outside. Everything inside the campus was orderly, clean, and serene. I had experienced two completely different-yet-exhilarating introductions to India, all in one day! One was stimulation for the senses and the other was stimulation for the soul. The combination of deep peace and powerful spiritual energy came over me when I was in Mt. Abu. I would wake up, without any alarm, between 2-3am. As someone who liked to sleep in, I wondered how I was waking up alert so early. I would meditate for two hours, picking the meditation room that I felt the most drawn to at that time. The result of having these early meditations before the crack of dawn was that I felt empowered, energized, and clear for the rest of the day.

After a week, while I was already enjoying the atmosphere and high energy in Mt. Abu, I had the experience of an immensely blissful connection during a three-hour collective meditation. It was clear to me that I was connecting with sacred energy, it was as if there was a line connecting myself with the Divine Source. Up until that point, God had still been a question mark. I knew that someone or something had been answering my heart's call, but I wasn't sure what that was. However, in those three hours, I felt a strong, and steady connection with a peace-filled, loving Source of Infinite Energy which was taking me beyond myself into the bodiless state. It felt as if I was drawn into a vortex with this Infinite Intelligence: soul-to-soul.

The next day, someone who had been in the same

room asked me if I knew that I was smiling for the whole duration of those three hours. I told him that I didn't know I was smiling externally, but that I could feel myself smiling subtly, internally – in bliss. After I felt the supersensuous joy of connecting with God's energy, I knew that all the experiences leading up to that moment had been God's responses to my heart's longing for truth.

I now know God as the most supportive being in my life. The one who is always there, steady and dependable; my cheerleader and loving parent who knows my potential, allows me to grow, and bolsters me when I need it the most. Over the last 15 years, I have had many experiences of God's peace, love, compassion, stability, wisdom, and bliss.

One particularly memorable evening, I became uncharacteristically sad. I couldn't figure out where this intensity of emotion had *suddenly* come from. It completely took over my mind. There was confusion, a sense of desperation, and feelings of isolation. I began expressing to God that I needed help to decipher what was going on. I suddenly felt myself in the bodiless state, being pulled towards radiating light and filled with limitless love. This love was the most tremendous and all-encompassing love I had ever experienced. It was so powerful that I wondered if I could handle it. I was in awe and trying to embrace the immensity of it. When I emerged from that experience, the sadness was gone entirely. I noticed the difference in my energy right away. And, I felt like myself again. I then understood that the immense sadness was not mine, but that I had picked it up from someone else. While being profoundly immersed in God's light and love, the negativity went out completely.

There have been countless other times that I have felt God's hug of peace or deep stability; letting me know that I am supported right where I am, as I am. Sometimes this support has come when I am actively trying to connect in meditation. At other times, it happens when I need it the most or when I am having a heart-to-heart conversation with the One. I am so happy I investigated the mystery of God with an open mind and heart. This relationship has become a constant reminder for me of my worth and potential.

I get sentimental recalling these experiences, and the way this beautiful relationship opened during my first trip to India. Being in Mt. Abu was like landing in a parallel, yet more heavenly, reality. It was a model of what is possible when souls are in touch with their original divine nature. I was encountering a culture of people whose lives were dedicated to making the world a more loving and peaceful place. Being immersed in so much kindness, day in and day out, was the dream of my heart coming to life.

When I was around ten years old, I told my mom that I wanted my allowance ($5 a week) to go towards supporting a child in Africa. She agreed and sent my allowance to a little girl, one whom I could write to and who could write back to me. I felt so happy looking at her photo on the fridge, knowing that she was able to use the money for school and whatever supplies she needed.

When I was a young teenager, my Grandpa took me and my cousin Andrew on a road trip. Andrew and I talked about creating a world where there would be an atmosphere of generosity, unity, and inclusivity; one in which there would be no need for money. This ideal world would use a bartering system that could provide equally well for everyone. We envisioned a world devoid of greed, separation, and lack.

Then, when I was twenty-one, I had a dream to adopt a house full of children that needed a safe and loving place to land. I wanted to provide them unlimited nurturing and support so that they could go out to make their great contributions in the world. As an adult, I realized that we are all children who need love, and that I could be most helpful by loving the inner child within everyone – even the adults.

Going to Mt. Abu showed me that my lifelong desire for there to be a world that operated out of pure love, care, and belonging was not only possible, but was actually happening. If there was already a model of it, then it was possible.

What I had dreamed about, I was experiencing on a vast scale for the first time. There was a secret to be learned at the Brahma Kumaris campus in Mt. Abu: they were operating in alignment with the subtle laws of the universe. There was so much care and natural abundance in everything. People were fed generously; there were even departments for sweet and salty snacks, in which you could go and pick up as much as you like (without having to get out a wallet). It was so freeing and felt so right. They were operating on the principles of selfless generosity and spiritual love. And everyone who came was so touched that they wanted to support this extraordinary place.

There was also so much service happening at their J Watumull Global Hospital, which I was naturally interested in because of my background in holistic health. I was touched by how much allopathic, homeopathic, and naturopathic medical care they were providing the residents in the surrounding villages at little to no cost; including countless eye surgeries, orthopedic surgeries, and many other basic but important services like dental work. I was able to assist in taking food to children in neighboring villages who didn't have much. I loved that there was care and humanity at every step.

My trip to Mt. Abu was changing me profoundly. It deepened my understanding of how to meditate and fill up with limitless amounts of pure energy. I felt more stable, peaceful, joyful, powerful, light, and free. It solidified my trust and ability to connect with the Divine Source – my eternal and loving parent.

All the goodness that I believed was possible to do in the world was possible and even better than what I imagined. God's skillful responses to my heart's longing guided me home to my soul, my spiritual family, and a restored faith that there can be a world motivated by noble qualities. More than just theory or hope, I now had consistent experiences of myself as a spiritual being, God as my supportive companion and a world of magnanimity based on elevated principles.

We all have different avenues which help us to know and understand ourselves and God's love. For me, it was 100% honest communication from the heart. When I didn't know if a Divine Source of Infinite Intelligence existed, my conversation was, "Whatever you are, if you are, show me the way." I learned that, when the heart of the child calls, our eternal parent cannot help but respond and guide us home to ourselves.

4

Into the Depths, I Go

Oh what a child am I
Got a feather and thought I could fly
When I came down, nearly drown
You lifted me to your eyes

I realized that the spiritual journey I had embarked upon would be an ever-evolving process. I stayed dedicated to my meditation practice, understanding deeper spiritual knowledge, and serving wherever I could. There were both huge and incremental shifts within myself and how I interacted with the world. I had noticeably more self-respect, patience, inner power, stability, and trust. Based on what I now understood about the divine nature of life, there didn't seem to be anything more critical than embodying the love, peace, wisdom, and bliss that I knew was possible within myself – and in the world.

Studying spiritual knowledge increased my understanding of the natural laws of the universe, like karma (whatever we give out will always return). As a practical lesson in karma, I saw that when I served from the heart, the result was always a wave of happiness that came back, surrounding me with pure joy. I noticed that when I lived from benevolence, every need was amply provided for. I didn't need to think about receiving anything when I focused on giving. I was learning how to live in alignment with the natural laws of the universe, in a cycle of good.

In the first decade of my spiritual journey, I reached a place where I felt extremely loved, supported, uplifted, and content in my relationship with God and myself. However, I could sense that a new phase was coming in my life. Around that time, some old emotions began resurfacing within me. These emotions took me by surprise because I thought I had worked through them, in counseling, during high school and college. Why were these old feelings rearing their ugly heads to cause me pain yet again?

I tried various things to work through these inconvenient feelings, like talking with someone new in a counseling capacity, working with my inner child, and journaling. But, when the feelings weren't defusing, I began to feel stuck. Although I felt great when I meditated, I still had unresolved emotions to deal with later. It became difficult to stay on track with what I needed to do, day-to-day, as I found myself daydreaming and procrastinating. I was becoming immobilized and unable to flow through the day as I had so easily before. I needed to find a solution that would allow me to deeply untangle the cords of mangled emotions from wherever they were originating. It was frustrating to not be in the happy-go-lucky space I had been in for almost a decade. But I had learned by now that if I put my honest effort into something and didn't give up, eventually I would be guided to a method that worked.

Around the same time, I was in school to learn several holistic health modalities. One afternoon, after doing a practice bodywork session on a friend, she offered to open the Akashic Records for me. She described it as an energetic record of the soul – past, present, and future – which is thought to be a compendium of all human events, thoughts, words, and emotions that *have* ever happened or *will* happen.

It was something I had not heard of before but was open to trying. She opened the record by reciting a prayer. I felt an immediate switch of energy, similar to the space I would enter in meditation, which was deeply silent and still. She saw several images, which she described for me in detail, along with sharing the specific information she was getting.

One of the images was of a checkerboard which was split in half. One side of the checkerboard had regular black and white squares, and the other side had colorful squiggly shapes that fit together like a puzzle. She said I was moving from the linear black and white squares ... to the side that was more colorful; and that I would be playing the same game, only in a different way. She also saw people waiting for me on a piece of land just beyond a river. She said these were "my people," whom I would be joining soon. The last thing she told me was that I would be entering into a destined spiritual partnership, which I did not have a choice about. It would be a partnership that was not just for the two of us, but for the good of something greater than us. I was skeptical because, even though I felt a new phase of my life was fast approaching, I didn't want my life to change in any major way.

I went about my life, doing the things that sustained me spirituality and trying to work with the emotions that were bubbling up. It was a challenging time. I longed to understand what was happening within me, but couldn't decipher it. Since I was in school for holistic health studies at that time, I tried to see if I could pinpoint the energetic causes of my fluctuating emotions. Whatever I tried helped a little, but they were band-aids, not full-on relief.

Almost eight months after my friend opened the Akashic Records, I was at a meditation retreat in New York. One day, during a break between sessions, I was asked to sit at a large table in the main hall, while I was waiting for someone with whom I had to do some work. There was one more person sharing the table; when I glanced over at him, I realized it was Vivek Kashyap. We had met several times in the past and had even facilitated a retreat together.

He told me that he was studying for a heart-centered coaching exam, in a modality known as Heart IQ, which he had been training extensively in for over two years. Interested in all things healing, my ears perked up. However, after just a few minutes, it was time to go work on the project I had originally come to do.

The next night, Vivek asked me if I wanted to finish our conversation. He could tell that I was interested in what he was learning and thought maybe it would be helpful for me. He shared that, even though he had gained so much from his meditation practice of over 20 years, he realized that he needed to add something to his practice that was explicitly designed for emotional healing. Vivek had researched coaches and training programs, and had found Christian Pankhurst's Heart IQ and Tej Steiner's Heart Circle to be the most compelling methods of healing. He began the Heart IQ coaching program with Christian and joined some Heart Circles with Tej. These heart-centered methods were not only helping him to understand his own emotions, but he was also learning how to benefit others through these processes. He was excited about combining his knowledge of meditation with these powerful methods of healing the heart, in order to create more authentic connection with others.

Before we left the retreat, Vivek offered to do some distance coaching with me, as he had to have several practice clients. Maybe working with him could provide insight into the emotions that had been stifling me, and enable me to move forward. It was worth a try. I had already utilized everything else I had at my disposal, but my issues had not been resolved.

During the first session, Vivek explained that a fundamental principle of healing is "what you can feel you can heal;" and that what often needs to be felt are a variety of difficult emotions (hurt, grief, fear) that have been unconsciously suppressed, in order for us to survive. He said that, between the stories, projections, and unsafe experiences of the past, the mind creates sophisticated defense mechanisms that prevent us from feeling the very things we *need* to feel – to heal. In other words, the mind and ego are programmed to avoid pain. It all seemed like sound logic to me.

As we did the Heart IQ heart-centered coaching, it was as if a secret vault which housed feelings of sadness, frustration, loss, and abandonment (primarily related to my mother's and aunt's deaths) was uncovered. The more vulnerable and real I allowed myself to become, the further we could pinpoint what was keeping my heart closed. I could feel that I was in a judgment-free zone with Vivek. His caring and calm demeanor was disarming, which allowed me to be 100% real with my feelings. He created a safe space and guided me – energetically and emotionally – to feel my way through the layers of past, unhealed experiences that were still subconsciously affecting me.

Being gently guided to open up places that had been shut down since childhood – and make connections with the parts of myself that had been long-buried – made me realize how powerful this method of coaching was. I saw immediate benefits, and they far surpassed any therapy I had done in the past. There was no need to recount my story verbally. We went directly to where the emotions and energy were being stored, and I learned how to embrace them. It was the opposite of suppression. It took me out of my head and allowed me to feel where the unintegrated energy was trapped, and then reintegrate it into my system from a place of acceptance. We unraveled the pain with loving attention.

After the heart-centered coaching sessions, he invited me to take part in a healing heart circle with a few others. Vivek created a safe container by taking us through a stepwise process that allowed us to be completely real and vulnerable. The circle provided undivided attention for each individual as they went through the coaching process with Vivek. Through the heart circle, I learned how kindred the human experience can be, and how healing it is for the self when we witness others heal.

It allowed us to digest our fear, pain, confusion, and shame together, thus creating a collective healing space for everyone so that no individual had to struggle alone. I noticed this helped in unburdening the individual more quickly; whereas embarking on the process of healing by oneself is often an enormous and lengthy endeavor.

I began to witness how much transformation happened within me as we became present, real, and heart-centered together. There was a mirroring of healing happening, and it never ceased to amaze me how much I was learning and growing each week. Within the group, people were opening up places deep inside that they hadn't allowed themselves to access for a very long time. With the usual masks of safety removed, everyone was discovering not only what was holding them back, but their voice and power which were just underneath them. The role of the facilitator was to create a safe container and help people navigate their way through their feelings. Vivek was naturally intuitive and skilled in guiding us to access the long-buried seeds of pain and disconnection. He helped us to stay in the heart and not shift into the stories in our head (thereby avoiding our feelings). Heart Circle work was the most profound emotional healing tool I had ever experienced.

Through the Heart Circle process, I learned that the trauma I experienced in the past, needed to be healed in the present. It had to be healed at the emotional *and* energetic levels *in the presence of other people.* To re-create trust with people, I needed to feel safe enough to let my tenderest places be received, knowing that they had a soft place to land. Through this process, I was able to heal parts of my heart that I hadn't even known were shut down – and were driving my behavior on a subconscious level. The anxiety I had been feeling about these unresolved feelings melted away as I healed.

Being witnessed and supported by others helped me embrace the parts of myself which were previously too painful to feel, and allowed me to reclaim and embody them to move forward in my journey of wholeness. Who would have thought that healing for the individual was exponentially increased when done collectively in a heart-centered space with others?

When I saw that healing was happening, not only for the individual who was taking the space to heal, but for the entire group, I understood the magic and necessity of healing collectively. It was showcasing that we cannot heal the trust issues we have with others, if we cannot open up and allow ourselves to become vulnerable. That which was disconnected and shut down in the heart, because it had been hurt, could only be repaired through unconditional love and support in the presence of others.

We truly are mirrors and medicine for each other. The way to wholeness and harmony, within ourselves, with others, and on the planet, is through collective healing.

We are not on this earth alone, but always in relationships of some kind. Connections create and sustain life. Spirituality is about creating deeply trusting and supportive connections with ourselves, God, and other beings. All of these places should feel 100% safe and supportive. As I learned to *really* open my heart to others, it helped me to heal myself more deeply than I knew I could. Opening my heart to give and receive love completely was the beautiful and necessary next step in my journey to trust.

Although it is beneficial to be on our own for periods of time, it can also limit our growth. This is especially true in terms of healing the parts of ourselves that have been hurt previously in relationships. If we isolate ourselves, we will not regain the capacity to have supportive connections. Heart-centered and open-hearted connections with others are imperative for life and growth. We all need to be touched by love and care daily. Love is what generates compassion, cooperation, and belonging. If we cannot give and receive love, because the heart is shut down, then we are missing out on a vital part of life.

Many types of relationships can help us feel loved and supported, as long as they are a safe space in which we can relax and be ourselves. If our heart is shut down or the walls are still up, we are not truly connecting with others. Relationships in which we can be vulnerable and real help us to trust others again. Trusting others enough to open our hearts and be able to be ourselves completely, free of judgment, is the only way we can create a world of trust. We have to know when it is time for us to be on our own, and also when it is time to be vulnerable within relationships with each other.

I learned how to trust myself and life again with God. I learned how to trust love and relationships again with Vivek and my beautiful friends. The deep healing of the heart I did has allowed me to be in a trusting and meaningful partnership with Vivek; which has shown me what pure, unconditional love looks and feels like. We all need people in our lives that help us to feel, know, and trust in the nurturing power of healthy relationships.

We all have different methods that will work for us when it comes to opening our hearts and creating deeply trusting relationships with others. The Heart IQ, heart-centered coaching and Heart Circle work, I did with Vivek, worked for me. I went from having impenetrable walls, made up of the fear of vulnerability and unsafety in personal relationships (because I never wanted to experience loss again), to being able to feel complete safety and trust in supportive and growth-enhancing connections.

Vivek was teaching meditation, mindfulness, and assisting people through their emotional blockages with heart-centered coaching, retreats, and heart circles; while I was teaching meditation and helping people align themselves spiritually, energetically, and physically through my holistic health coaching practice. We combined the best of what we had learned in these different areas of healing, and began to naturally come into contact with others who were looking for alternative ways to heal their deep-seated emotions. Fortunately, we could share from a broader range of tools we had acquired, which were helping us tremendously. We now knew from first-hand experience that if we ignore even one area of wellbeing, it will come up for healing at some point.

I have seen that there are only two things to fear in the process of healing: the fear of vulnerability, and rigidness in my thinking. Both of these are barriers to the healing that needs to take place. The ego is the part of us that is rigid and afraid to be vulnerable. That is why we have to be smart and find ways to sneak past the ego ... so that we can heal all the aspects of our Self deeply.

Openness and vulnerability are the doors we *must* walk through, which we reach when we are ready to make big and lasting changes. They have allowed me to try unexpected routes, moving me towards more freedom, connection, and joy. Letting go of having to control everything, just to keep myself safe, is the best thing I have ever done.

In this ever-evolving journey towards health, harmony and balance, I have seen that we usually need several different approaches to cover all the aspects of the self that need TLC (tender loving care). Becoming open to new methods of healing, enabled me to trust in the magic of life again. I saw first-hand that help showed up in unexpected ways which expanded my heart, deepened my understanding of the self, and healed the areas in need of attention. We each have a unique path of healing which we can be guided along, and it's comforting to know that we don't have to figure it out all by ourselves.

5

Healing in the Subtle Realm

There is no end to your love
Sweeping in, touching me, my Beloved
And even when I am not seeking
But there is a need that you're seeing
You send angels on the wings of a dove

I have always had an interest in natural healing, and have taken several courses over the years in various holistic health modalities. Some of those modalities work with the emotional and energetic causes of physical ailments. In my experiences with Reiki and Polarity Therapy, and later through Heart IQ, I have seen that we can carry blocked energy and suppressed emotions for as long as is necessary – for us to survive.

If we are not able to process an event when it happens, it gets stored in our system energetically – as if in a safety deposit box – until we find a supportive environment in which we can face it. The energy of pain, abuse, abandonment, rejection, correction, and fear does not just disappear. As we know from the first law of thermodynamics, energy can neither be created nor destroyed ... it is transferred and transformed. It's just a matter of when and how. We can either feel and heal it now, or feel and heal it later.

Just as I discovered that emotions and experiences from this life can be suppressed and pop up down the road; so, too, I found that the body and subtle body can hold onto these things throughout more than one lifetime. Although the personal healing experiences I'm going to share here are hard to describe, I think they are worth making an effort to convey. They illustrate how the subtle and physical bodies can create illness and injury, based on past trauma and suppressed energy, in order for us to heal it. They also show that we are divinely supported in our healing journeys, and in ways that we least expect it.

I needed two ligament repair surgeries in the last couple of years, one on each ankle. After finding a doctor willing to repair an old injury proved tough, I was referred to a surgeon who specializes exclusively in ankles (and one who was more than sure that they could be fixed): Alexis Dixon, M.D. She made me feel completely at ease and confident about the process. I was in the best hands and would be relieved to get what had become a long-standing issue resolved.

Before having these surgeries, I thought the pain and instability in my ankles traced back to nothing more than a badly torn ligament and a few ankle sprains. Since I assumed a physical injury was responsible for the pain and subsequent issues with my ankles, it never crossed my mind that these physical challenges could stem from suppressed emotions, stuck energy, or past traumatic experiences. Thus, these profound healing experiences both surprised and captivated me.

Following each of my surgeries (which were both very successful), I learned firsthand and in dramatic fashion about the supportive, healing power of divine energy. In each instance, when these healing experiences happened, I was in severe pain which was not fully relieved by the pain medication. The first time this happened, on my right ankle, my close friend Marcela was visiting. I had the thought to ask her to put her hands on the surgical ankle for just a few minutes, to see if her loving energy would help to ease my discomfort. I expected this to simply be a few minutes of positive vibrations for the ankle, to help me sleep with less pain.

We were caught off guard when intense healing energy started pouring through her hands. It was similar to Reiki, only much stronger than I had ever felt. There was so much energy that it felt as if her hands were glued to my splint through a downward vibrational force.

From the knee down, my right leg felt like it had been wrapped in a cloud-like cocoon, and I could not feel the pain anymore. It was like there had been an anesthetic application. After a period of initial soothing, the pain came back with very specific sensations. I started to feel extreme pain inside the ankle joint, along with an intense sensation of fire going down the lateral side of my foot (from my ankle to the ends of the little toe and the toe next to it).

The entire splint was burning up, so much so that Marcela was sweating from the heat. The pain and heat were almost too much to bear and continued to intensify. Because of the volume of energy coming through her hands, I realized that we were experiencing some kind of a healing phenomenon. Even though staying present with this pain was difficult, Marcela and Vivek (who had come into the room when he heard me cry out) began to support and guide me through the process. With their encouragement, I leaned into the increasing pain and heat, instead of resisting it.

They suggested I check myself energetically and emotionally to see what was moving. I found that there were feelings of sadness and loss in my navel area, which felt related to my mom. Once I allowed myself to fully feel the emotions that were coming up, the pain slowly began to decrease and, eventually, the entire area calmed down.

My entire lower leg, knee to toes, became wrapped in that cloud-like sensation again. It felt like a second round of subtle anesthesia was applied, and that I had just had another surgery; only this one was subtle, energetic, and I was awake for it. The process took an hour and a half, almost the same length as my actual surgery. To my surprise, that anesthetic feeling did not go away. I was in a pain-free state and didn't need to take another pain pill for thirty hours! Compare that to every two hours that I was having to take it before, which wasn't alleviating the pain way anyway. After this healing experience, I only needed the pain medication once every 24-30 hours, for a week.

A very similar thing happened on my left ankle a year and a half later, when I was incredibly fortunate to have my dear friend Michelle come to care for me post-surgery. It was similarly around a week after my surgery, and I was experiencing heightened pain that day. I asked her if she would hold my left ankle for a few minutes before we went to sleep, in an attempt to rest with less pain. The same sequence occurred, with an enormous amount of potent energy coming through her hands. This time though, the initial soothing anesthetic sensation lasted thirty minutes, roughly twenty more minutes than the first time it happened. I was relieved, as it seemed that this ankle only needed the divine healing energy and that there would be nothing to process like the last time.

However, that absence of pain didn't last. Suddenly, I had the sensation of a thick, metal shackle clamped around the top of my left ankle, which seemed to be cutting off all circulation to my foot! Sure enough, when Michelle touched my toes, they were ice-cold. The tightening pain and ice-cold sensation continued to increase to an almost unbearable point.

I remembered that the main thing which seemed to help last time was to embrace it – not resist it. As I checked what was moving subtly in my system, I felt knotted energy in my solar plexus. I leaned into it and expressed the emotions, of being trapped and powerless, that felt associated with it. As I did this, the squeezing and loss of circulation sensations increased, but eventually they started to decrease.

Michelle began physically sweeping the energy away, which also seemed to help release it. After all was said and done, my leg was completely pain-free and back in that cloud-like cocoon. There was no more pain at all, and I *never* had to take another pain pill again. I went from taking them every four hours, to *not at all*!

The way this divine healing energy took away the pain and reduced the pain pills I needed – by 90% on the right side and 100% on the left side – was mind-bogglingly awesome. What had we just experienced, and who was doing it?! It certainly wasn't pleasant, but it was obviously necessary; and a real gift.

I'm so thankful to Marcela and Michelle for being open and receptive to these deep and unexpected healing experiences. They were loving, intuitive, and powerful enough to stay present through what turned into long and intense healing sessions. My experience of working with Vivek through the Heart IQ method had prepared me to know how to be present with the pain and feel through all the emotions (something I wouldn't have known to do before).

These healing gifts enticed me to want to understand more the multi-layered, multi-sensory, time-spanning nature of the soul's experience and how it impacts matter. I can no longer look at *anything* that's happening with the body as something isolated to just the physical plane, or limited to one-time frame. The experiences of the fire/heat and the shackle/cold were so tangible and real. Were these mysterious feelings and pains the energetic and emotional remnants from this, or another, lifetime? Although I am not sure where they fall on the timeline, they were too real not to have happened along the soul's journey somewhere in time.

These experiences taught me even more deeply that matter is responding to our consciousness, energy, and emotions. Only when our consciousness is at its healthiest can we support matter to thrive and vibrate with vitality. If emotions or traumatic experiences are left unhealed, we can carry them across time and store them in our energy field. Then, in order to be released and healed, they can show up in this or our next physical body in the form of illness or injury.

Even though it was tough at the moment, I am grateful for these profound and challenging experiences with my ankles. Not just because it relieved the pain when nothing else could and showed me a whole other level of emotional and energetic healing; but because they made me realize – even more – how supported we are by the Divine in our healing journey. There is comfort in knowing that our healing is supported in ways that we do not know and haven't even fathomed yet. I have seen that healing at all levels of the self – spiritual, mental, emotional, physical, and energetic – is important and supported both by God and life.

6

The Death of Death

I am not the encapsulation of this body
But the spiritual dweller within
Do not confuse me with this name, form or skin
We will always be together as eternal kin
And never apart because I am close to your heart

I want to share another spiritual experience, which
wholly transformed my experience of death. It created
a deeper understanding of the soul and the continuation
of our loving connections with each other. It also
revealed to me how beautiful the experience of leaving
our bodies has the potential to be, especially when we
have worked on ourselves spiritually.

My close friend, Bebe Butler, was a fellow Raj
Yogi who had been on the spiritual path for over 20
years. She was one of the most real, wise, kind, open,
and entertaining souls I have ever known and was like
a sister to me. She was extremely loved and full of
many creative gifts which she shared generously with

the world. As a gifted artist, she painted in pictures and words her experience of beauty, divinity, and silence. She taught others how to connect deeply with their authentic self through art. As a puppeteer, she created children's puppet shows (props and all) to give entertaining experiences and share valuable lessons through story. As a meditation teacher, she had a way of making meditation both practical and magical at the same time. She kindly guided almost a hundred online inspirational meditations that people can easily follow. To her family, friends, students, co-workers – and all who knew her – she was a true angel.

Some of the words from one of the paintings she made, particularly reminds me of her: "When there are no answers, trade your questions for sweet solitude. Answers rarely come because you force them to. When silence and divine timing collide, answers emerge as inevitably as the sunrise. So go and be still."

In the last year of her life, while Bebe was going through her second bout with cancer, I had the opportunity to stay with her twice. Both times she was resilient, calm, and brave. All who loved her hoped and believed that she would recover. She was trying to heal herself through various allopathic and naturopathic methods. But, if for some reason, she was supposed to move on from this life and into the next chapter of her story, she accepted that. She trusted her eternal journey, as a soul, and simply wanted to be where she could give the most benefit.

The first time I stayed with her, I had gone to help

her pack up her apartment because she was going to stay with her dad while she was in treatment. One day, we took a stroll (with her calico kitty Bella in a pink cat stroller) down to a very sweet river and sat underneath a big oak tree. The breeze off the water stirred the leaves above our heads. We decided it was a perfect spot to meditate. Bebe invited me to repeat after her the lines of a powerful prayer that had been an important part of her healing journey. I made a recording of us reciting the prayer, which I still listen to sometimes. It went:

> *Spirit that I am,*
> *I invite you to remove*
> *everything that is no longer part of my highest good*
> *and service in the world;*
> *please do this as gently as possible;*
> *and put me in the place*
> *and around the people*
> *where I can find my most joyful way of living and giving;*
> *where I can fulfill my destiny of being in this world*
> *and being an instrument for the highest task;*
> *please do this now,*
> *thank you.*

A couple of months later, while she was undergoing holistic treatment in Arizona, I was able to stay with her for a few weeks. We had lots of adventures while I was there. One time, an unexpected surgery put her in the hospital for five days. She was in pain, but still wanted to read a spiritual book that someone had given her. As

I was reading it out loud to her, we both had a wonderful experience of lightness and laughed for more than half an hour. It was so healing; we felt that the laughter itself was divinely inspired.

When it was time for me to return home, Bebe asked if I would come to Florida to visit her again around Thanksgiving. We made plans and talked about how we could spend a long weekend doing nurturing and pampering things – together with a couple of our close friends who are also in the healing field. Everyone liked this idea, so we bought our tickets well in advance and were looking forward to having a Bebe healing party. We planned to gather around her and give her all the love, reiki, massage, and play that she could handle.

Just two weeks before our scheduled visit, I received a call from her father. He told me that she had taken a sudden turn for the worse and he didn't know if she would still be there by the time we arrived. Tears rolled fast down my cheeks, as I allowed myself to feel the sadness without pushing it away.

I wanted to go to Florida, but I knew that Bebe's family would want to be with her. I decided to be supportive by sending Reiki and doing meditation for her in the morning, evening, and on my lunch break at work. I was surrounding her with light and meditating for an easy and peaceful transition. A part of me wished she would still be there when we arrived in ten days, but I didn't want her to suffer for even a moment.

Two days after her father called me, I was concentrating on a technical spreadsheet at the end of a long workday, when I was struck suddenly by a feeling of bliss *all* around me. I paused, noticing the significant shift in energy, and looked up from my paperwork towards the computer. It said 4:24 p.m. on the clock. The time caught my attention because it was the month and day of Bebe's birth, 4/24. Seeing repetitive number patterns, like 11:11, was something that had been happening with me for several years (which Bebe knew). After seeing the clock, I understood that the intense bliss, which was a combination of supersensuous joy and freedom, must be her!

This feeling lasted until it was time to leave, 35 minutes later. I got in the car and began a conversation with Bebe; so naturally, as if she was right there in the passenger seat. I specifically remember talking to her about what I was feeling and how amazing it was. When I reached home, as soon as I got in the door, I sat down to meditate for her. All the while, I was smiling because I was still immersed in that heavenly feeling of bliss.

Nearly two hours from the time I first felt the blissful energy around me, I received a text informing me that Bebe had left the body. I could not be sad – not even a little bit – because I could feel the fantastic, liberated space she was in. This beautiful experience continued for another two hours.

The service for Bebe, held at the meditation center, was standing-room-only. I began to get teary-eyed during the slideshow of Bebe's life, especially when some of the pictures I had taken the last time I was with her flashed on the screen. It was bringing back those beautiful final moments and memories. But, as the first few tears rolled down, I felt a quiet message in my heart: "Remember what I showed you." I was instantly reminded that she was in a truly liberated and joyful state, and that I didn't need to be sad.

The following week, I was able to find a moment alone with Bebe's parents. I asked them what time she had left the body. They told me that it happened at the same time I initially felt her at work, 4:24 p.m. PST, which was almost two hours before I received the news that she had passed. I felt so thankful to have learned, through her, that it's possible to leave the body in such a bliss-filled state. It was such a gift for me to know that she was in a joyful place, and on to her next adventure. It helped me trust even more in the benevolent process of birth and death – the accuracy of the timing of when we come and go.

In the months and year that followed, I experienced other moments when I felt her connecting with me. They were all unexpected things that could have only been her. I will share one here: At the time when Vivek and I were trying to figure out the last exercise of a retreat we were facilitating at Anubhuti Retreat Center, Bebe vividly appeared to me in a dream. She walked me through an unfamiliar exercise, *step-by-step*. It would be the perfect way to access power for the participants and to finish the retreat with exuberance. She knew just what we needed to do, to accomplish the experience of people stepping into their power and joy. We used her exercise in the retreat. That exercise turned out to be the favorite part of the retreat for most of the participants.

In those sweet moments of connection over the first year, I was letting go of who she had been and feeling excited about her journey forward. She was (and is) a most generous, creative, kind, and joyful soul. She loved to see others happy. Even at her departure, she wanted others to know what a liberated state she was in. I know she took her joyful, ecstatic, pure energy with her into the next phase of her journey ... flying on the wings of bliss and freedom.

As you can imagine, this was very different than my previous experiences with death. Before, there had been so much sadness, along with lots of confusion and questions of "why?" She transformed a sad and confusing process into one of comfort and pure joy. Who could have thought that leaving the body could be such a beautiful experience? Of course, over her 20 years of Raja Yoga meditation, Bebe had done a lot of work on herself. Leaving in that state of bliss didn't happen without any effort. She was consistent with her daily meditation practice and lived a generous life of service; both of which helped her to make her transition out of the body in that way. It seemed to me that she was in a very trusting space, both within and without the body – a space of deep spiritual awareness and freedom.

I witnessed how she kept up with her meditation and made time for silence, even in the most challenging times (like when she was in the hospital). She handled everything through the strength of her spirituality, which gave her a great deal of trust in life. She had a real, tangible, and enjoyable relationship with God.

There's another essential lesson I learned by experiencing her in that post-body blissful state. As Bebe was going through her treatment, she was focused not only on her physical health, but also on her spiritual, emotional, and energetic well-being. This situation was creating a reason and the time for her to heal deeper aspects within herself. She used that time to care for herself on *all* the different levels.

I've seen through both her cancer process and my surgical healing process, that when we get extra time to nurse ourselves because of illness or injury, it's because we need to heal things on deeper levels. It's preparing us to move forward to what is next, in a healed and upgraded state. Then we are ready for a fresh start; whether that is in the same body, or in the next one. In either case, we take our healing with us.

With Bebe's amazing transition, I understood more clearly, that our parts in the drama of life never stop. We continue to play on like a band that never gets tired or a song that never gets old. We are the eternal music, the spirit within, which has come into form. When we cultivate the wealth of the Self, it comes with us: our virtue, vibrations, good karma, and character. The happiness received becomes equal to what we have given. It is a cycle of good. And the more in alignment with our divine nature our hearts and intentions are, the more we ride on the waves of happiness and love.

When we can trust the sacred interconnected nature of life, as Bebe did, then we are in very joyful territory where we feel incredibly supported by it all. That is liberation. And we don't have to wait to leave the body to feel it!

Part II

Effect

7

Magical to Practical

When I think about these experiences, I am reminded of how enchanting, intriguing, and magical life can be when we are tuned into the absolute wonder of it all. Thank you for allowing me to share them with you. As you know, I started this journey from a place of bewilderment, not knowing what or who I could trust anymore. Ironically, that which was the most incomprehensible seemed like the most trustworthy source at the time.

I decided to surrender to what I didn't know – and I'm so glad I did! Because, instead of living with so much doubt and confusion, I now move through the world with a deep-seated trust in life.

Everything difficult that happened in my life caused me to search deeply within myself and always stay open to new possibilities. Because of the wondrous experiences and discoveries that followed, I know for certain that:

I'm a soul;
God is lovingly there as my guide;
Everything in life is beneficial;
Others are my mirrors and my medicine;
This body is my faithful companion;
And the soul's journey continues ...

... as do our loving connections with each other. These are things I *know* because knowledge of them came through direct experiences. Nothing could make me doubt them! It is so liberating to have trust in all these areas because I can relax, be held, and embrace life more fully.

When the responses to my heart's mantra: "Whatever you are, if you are, show me the way," started to come, they seemed like something supernatural. Now I realize they are quite normal because we are multidimensional beings in a multidimensional universe. Previously, I saw life in 2D, when it is really a 4D show. Becoming open was the beginning of seeing the world through the 20/20 lenses of spiritual understanding. If I hadn't opened myself up and become vulnerable, I would not have experienced what I did or know what I do now. In other words, my third eye – the eye of awareness – might still be closed, and I may be caught up in my old stories and perceptions. That would have been sad, indeed! Because then I would only be seeing a fraction of reality and not the whole gamut of the soul's existence. I love understanding more deeply how all the dots connect in this wondrous thing called life!

I needed to have those otherworldly experiences of the incorporeal nature of myself, God, and others, as well as the interwoven perfection of life – so that I could find solid ground again. Sometimes people assume that, if someone is spiritually inclined, they are not "grounded." But in my experience, spiritual awareness grounded me back into the unlimited 100% safe, 100% stable eternal self; as opposed to that which is temporal and constantly changing.

My spiritual experiences became the solid ground from which I could grow exponentially. They allowed me to understand how to be in the world in a more integrated, free, and sustainable way. I found my ground in the sky. Knowing myself as the eternal soul opened so many doors for me, especially my mind and heart.

Some people don't need to have tangible spiritual experiences to know that they are souls and that life is supporting them. Some people came into life knowing that and haven't wavered. Then there are others, like me, who need everything to be proven to them through direct experiences; only then can they know and trust in the benevolent nature of life again. Either way, I have seen that it's always important to be open to that which we don't understand yet. That gives us a chance to try on new ideas and see if there is a better fit for us.

Do you believe in anything just because you were told it was true? Spirituality is about becoming grounded in truth and letting that guide your life. But, it has nothing to do with following something you have been told to do or believe. Once we have become deeply connected to the truth within ourselves, we need very few outside rules and regulations, because we are self-regulating.

Finding out that life is spiritual in nature was just the beginning for me. Those experiences were the door, but not the destination. I learned to walk down a new road, in a new way, with the awareness these experiences were affording me. I had new goals, too: to truly embody everything I was learning and realizing in meditation, and to live from the soul's divine potential.

Spirituality is not about having visions or being in a blissful state all the time. It's about being an everyday embodiment of virtues and becoming a source of benevolence on this planet. Spirituality is practical. It's living from the inside out as pure-hearted beings, using our bodies and making choices from the wisest part of ourselves for the highest good of all.

It is awareness of the natural laws that govern the universe. Spirituality enables us to understand the impact we have on ourselves, others, and our environment – down to what we are thinking and feeling. It's knowing how to use our mind and heart for the highest benefit. It is realizing the goodness that we are, and doing as many acts of kindness with it as possible. Spirituality is seeing how we can bring benefit to ourselves, our surroundings, and all sentient beings. It is causing no harm.

Living a spiritual life is to understand the law of karma at the *subtlest* levels, so we can see where we have been unconsciously creating karmic debt and inadvertently having to pay it back. It is becoming smarter so that we can make life work for us ... not book smart, but life smart!

It reminds us that we are capable of doing so much good when we are aware, and so much harm when we are not. It teaches us our responsibility to do the right thing and operate from mindful awareness. Spirituality educates us about our eternal spiritual nature and the finite nature of the body. It reveals that our inner transformation and our elevated actions are the only forms of wealth we can take with us. It teaches us how to be a loving master of our mind, emotions, bodies, and senses. It puts us back in the driver's seat so that we can make conscious and balanced choices for ourselves and the planet.

This spiritual awakening for me has not just been about knowing that I am a soul and that God exists, but also realizing how much I am like that One. As the parent, so the child. In my experience, God's primary role has been to remind me of my potential and show me how to imbibe divine virtues. I have learned that my relationship with God matures and is strengthened as I live my life with spiritual principles, self-respect, love, and humility.

Spirituality has taught me more virtuous ways of interacting with everything in my life. This has helped me to have more respectful relationships in every possible direction. I, the soul, have *relationships* with my mind, body, emotions, energy, others, God, nature, money, time, life, and even death. I can decide how symbiotic these relationships will be based on my intentions and choices.

Through spirituality, I have understood that there are invisible accounts I am creating, which are either accumulating debt or wealth. We are continually involved in a give-and-take of energy in these areas of interaction, but not always consciously. It means that those things in my life which have become relationships of bondage, from negative karmas done in the past, can become relationships of freedom and benevolence; as I create positive karma in the present, for now, and for the future.

I'm sure you have seen the law of karma working in your life. Sometimes it comes back right away, like a boomerang, and other times it comes back later. It always comes back, though! The more we become subtly aware of the clear connection between cause and effect, the more quickly we can determine the sources of harmony or conflict in our lives and make choices accordingly. Having spiritual knowledge and awareness helps us to course-correct after getting feedback from our actions, and choose that which is beneficial and for the highest good of all.

I have seen that relationships of trust are developed when the right effort is put in over time. Doing the right thing gives us energy and power. Trust is built with our self when, time and time again, we trust our intuition and choose that which is right over that which is just comfortable or easy. Trust is built with others when we are there for them unconditionally and trust their journey. Trust is built with God when we are honest and make sincere spiritual effort. Trust is built with our bodies when we respect and listen to them. Time and time again, when we do the right thing, we develop lasting self-respect and deep trust. We begin to see the cycles of goodness and pure action returning as power, love, peace, and happiness. This is spirituality!

As I said in the beginning, I've never felt the experiences I had were just for me. It has always been clear they were meant to be shared with others, too. The first six chapters were about the most eye-opening experiences in my life, which enabled me to trust in life again. In the remaining chapters, I will share some of the practical things I have learned throughout my spiritual journey about creating more supportive relationships of love and trust with myself, God, others, matter, and life.

I share these in case they come in handy for you on your journey, as well. Some of them may serve as a jumping-off point for you or a reminder along the well-trodden path that you have been on for a long time. I hope that they provide food for thought; and also leave plenty of space for your own realizations about how to strengthen the trust, love, harmony, and support in all the areas of relationship in your own life.

8

Creating a Relationship of Trust with #1

1 *A Lasting Relationship*

Every good relationship begins with getting to know someone. The more you get to know them, the closer the relationship becomes. Getting to know and creating a deeper relationship with ourselves means that we are continually learning new, awesome things about ourselves. And knowing ourselves paves the way for connecting with everyone and everything else in our lives.

All of us have the intrinsic qualities of being able to love, be happy, and be peaceful, along with many other innate virtues of the self. However, each of us is unique in the way that these qualities, and our energy, are comprised and expressed. We each have a unique "soul print," if you will. Even though we all have the same divine components, they are arranged in various synergistic blends. Similarly, our bodies are made up of the same elements; but we are all physically unique, having different fingerprints, facial features, body sizes, and so on.

To experience this, think about the energy you feel when you are around a certain person. Now, think of the energy you feel around a different person. Each person gives you a specific energetic experience when you are with them. We all have, and share with others, a unique energy because we are all unique souls. Each soul adds its own particular and important energy to the world!

Realizing the things that make you uniquely who you are directly impacts your ability to be fully expressed. The important thing is to get to know your distinctive attributes; only then will you know if you are being the most authentic expression of yourself. Finding ways to explore this, until you feel like you not only know yourself but deeply appreciate, love, and value who you are, is so important. Remember: no one else can bring into the world what you are meant to share, which means being fully expressed is vital. Getting to know ourselves in this way becomes an act of benevolence, because the more we are in touch with our true self, the more we will spread the fragrance of our unique energy and virtues.

There are so many ways to know our unique strengths and qualities. An important first step for me was getting to know myself as a spiritual being, beyond the space and time of a limited identity (based only on the body). Once I did that, it helped to deepen the relationship with myself because I was able to tap into more authentic and eternal aspects of who I am. Find the method that works best for you. For me, it was Raja Yoga Meditation. The time invested in getting to know, nurture, and love the self is always time well spent. This relationship is worth all the time and energy that it needs! After all, who will you be with forever? Who can never be separated from you? Who is your #1? **You are your #1.**

2 *Essential Silence Time*

How can we develop a deeper and more supportive relationship with ourselves if we don't spend enough quality time with ourselves? I'm not talking about Netflix and chilling, either. I mean time spent sans entertainment, people, work, messages, social media, or any other distractions. Quiet time – time out – is essential silence time (EST). You can also think of it as essential self-time. I have found that EST is necessary for me to have every day. Usually, the more I get, the better. There are so many ways to create this time. The main thing is to have nothing taking up space in the time which you have carved out to be with yourself.

Some ways that I make time to be with myself are meditation, journaling, or going for walks. Occasionally,

I get creative and paint. All of those activities are quiet and reflective; they allow me to connect more deeply with myself. We can each find creative ways – ways that best suit our tastes and styles – to get the most out of the time spent with ourselves. Just as long as it's quality time that we are spending.

Some might argue that watching TV is quality time. But let me ask you: If you're with another person and you're both watching TV, who are you connecting with more – the TV, or the other person? The TV takes up most of your attention. So, don't allow this to be the "quality time" you spend with yourself. That's entertainment time, which has its own place, too.

If media entertainment is the main way you spend most of your time with yourself, do an experiment, and don't watch it for a few days. Or, spend just half of the time you normally spend watching it. Spend more quality time with yourself – have some EST, and see what a difference it makes!

Entertainment can be an easy out, when we want to relax our mind and not think. It's especially tempting nowadays, because there are so many great shows to choose from. Never before in history has the variety of quality entertainment been so easily available, as it is now! However, if most of our free time alone is spent in front of the TV, then we are missing out on the chance to build the most important relationship of our lives.

For those who do not consider entertainment time to be their quality time with the self, here's another question: Are you getting *enough* quality time with yourself? Enough quiet time: silence time, reflection time, self-care and exploratory time? If not, try getting up earlier by the amount of time you need to make it possible. A common practice of those who meditate is to get up earlier to have quality, quiet time. You can do this, or you can find other pockets of the day where you can nurture and care for yourself. Perhaps you can find two 20-minute pockets (or several 5/10/15-minute ones) which, once you piece together, will add up to a solid, daily investment in the significant relationship with yourself.

You won't be disappointed, and probably never bored. If you do get bored, find a new way to spend that time. Make some special dates with yourself. It can be in the bath, at a park, in any corner of your house, or at the beach ... as long as your mind and heart are focused on being fully present with yourself. EST is any time spent upgrading, understanding, and nurturing yourself.

3 *Follow Your Heart*

Getting to know yourself more deeply and spending quality time with yourself will make it easier to hear the messages coming from within. Being able to listen to your inner guidance is required ... in order to create a relationship of total trust with the self.

As souls, we are all unique and have our own soul paths. No one's path can be just like another, just like no one's body can be exactly like another. Both the body and soul are unique, and so is the journey we each take. That means that the only person that knows our next right move is us. No one else can know what we need to do next to fulfill the mission and goals we have as a soul. Don't count on anyone else to tell you this. Look within yourself; your heart's longing will guide you to what you need to do next. As you may recall, at the beginning of my spiritual journey, I did not know what steps I needed to take next in my life. So, I did one simple thing: I followed my heart's longing to my next step.

Sitting there under that towel, on the beach, I felt a deep desire to know Truth and understand the purpose of life. It was a pure desire, deep within my heart, that led me to create the mantra, "Whatever you are, if you are, show me the way." It was that simple. I wasn't clear on ANYTHING at that point, except that I felt the longing in my heart to understand life's deeper truths. My heart's longing was the only thing pointing me in any direction, so I followed it.

Look at the result: following the pure longing in my heart created a line of energy, a path, between my longing and the answer. Following my heart set things into motion. It created an opening where I had been closed, and allowed the answers to be revealed to me in unprecedented ways. The pure longings in our heart are powerful guides that will not lead us astray.

That's why a huge component of trusting yourself

is to **listen to your heart – it knows the way.** Stop waiting for society or your family (or anyone else for that matter) to tell you what you should be, want, or do. They can only know what they need to be, want, and do. They can only hear the quiet guidance that directs their soul's journey throughout time, not yours. Only you can know what you need to do next to fulfill your soul's journey. Your heart is your GPS.

Sometimes, because of what others desire for us or try to pressure us into (in order to keep themselves comfortable), we suppress our heart's pure longing. Then we suffer a lot. Why do we suffer? Because, when we follow someone else's GPS and not our own, we are out of alignment with where we are going and the next step we are supposed to take. We feel this misalignment and, although we are moving, our inner brakes start screeching at us until we turn around. It doesn't feel good or right to go against the flow of where our path is meant to go. And that is for good reason!

How else would we ever get back on the path that we are meant to be on if we didn't get some kind of signal that we are going in the wrong direction? It can be in any situation, and with anyone: parents, bosses, friends, family, colleagues, social media "friends," church leaders, self-help gurus – even strangers. Do not comply out of fear. Whenever fear is dictating what we are doing, we are going in the wrong direction! Fear will lead us astray. But following our heart will guide us in the direction of our highest potential.

I am a prime example: towards the beginning of

my spiritual journey, some of the people in my family opposed it for various reasons. Some, because they didn't believe in God or what I was studying; and some, because I didn't believe in God from the same viewpoint that they did. I know that they thought they were trying to protect or save me, but do you know what I realized? I could not live my life for anyone else or live their version of the story. They had to live their lives and find what gave them the most happiness and peace, and I had to do the same. Only I knew what was next in my journey because only I could feel where my heart was guiding me. I had to protect and save myself by listening closely to what I needed to do for my soul's progress. And I am so glad I did.

Otherwise, I would not have had all these life-changing experiences, nor met many of the people that I love and respect so much. When I followed the guidance of the soul by feeling into my heart's true longing, everything began to fall into place. I have seen many times that when you follow your heart, others often come around. They eventually realize that you are happy and doing what *you* were meant to do.

In any case, even if they don't come around, don't base your decisions on other people's opinions in place of what you know, in your heart, you need to do. If you do, you will suppress the fulfillment and joy of your soul. Remember: no two people's paths are the same. Take time to listen in to the pure guidance from your heart, which is pointing you in the direction of what is next.

One word of caution in this: This is not guidance

from the head, which can be fueled by desires that come from ego, greed, attachment, or fear. If it is coming from your heart, it will be inherently good for you. It will make you feel grounded and peaceful, and it will take you towards your highest potential. You will feel from within that this is what has to happen next, for you to truly move forward in fulfilling what you are meant to do and be.

Once we realize that our heart is the GPS of the soul, we are far less likely to get lost; and we will move forward with wondrous results. When we end up at our right destination, again and again, we will learn to trust ourselves and our unique journey even more.

4 *Trust Your Intuition*

This piggybacks on #3 but also deserves its own highlight because it's so important. What is the difference between following your heart and trusting your intuition? Both of them depend on the capacity to listen to the guidance coming from within. In my experience, the heart speaks in longings, usually pulling me towards a new destination; like when I feel strongly that something has to happen next in my life to move forward. Intuition, on the other hand, often says "yes" or "no" to things on the spot. It tells me what I should do, and if something is good for me or not, usually right before it's about to happen. Intuition is the inner compass, which points to my true north (living in alignment with my highest values), and it lets me know if I am still heading in the right direction. It says deal or no deal.

Intuition is the instinctive knowing that protects our journey and keep us in alignment with our truth. This quiet (and sometimes loud) part of us lets us know if something is right for us or not, without us having to reason it out consciously. Intuition can work in the form of doubt, too, when we don't feel sure about something. A good rule of thumb is: When in Doubt ... Don't, or, When in Doubt ... Wait it Out.

Some people ask how they can tell the difference between their intuition and thoughts coming from their mind. I notice that when signals come from my intuition (inner knowing), I am not using my energy to produce them, i.e., there is no thinking required. It emerges naturally, flows effortlessly, and is completely clear. When something comes from your inner knowing, it is accompanied by feelings of calmness and stability. Whereas the mind doesn't just know, it thinks and tries to figure things out; it debates, questions, and wonders. It is always deducing, calculating, and trying to choose what to do next. Its energy *can* be peaceful, but it can also be so many other things: harried, hurried, and worried.

In my experience, when we are living in a soul-aware, soul-conscious state, we are living from our intuition. We enter a feeling-based space where we are more aware, get into a flow, and can sense what needs to be done next, without having to *think* about it. Again, the heart is like a GPS, showing us through its pure longings, how to reach our destination, step-by-step. Our intuition is like a compass, letting us know if we are heading in the right direction, and are in alignment with our truth, at every given moment.

Both of these subtle muscles have to be *used*. If we don't exercise them, they weaken. If we do, they get stronger. We want them to be strong because they are our guides. I have never regretted following my intuition or heart's pure longings, but I have regretted *not* following them – out of fear, someone's influence or opinion. Realize that only you can know and take the steps that will lead you to your greatest potential. Those steps can only be guided from within. No one else can take those steps for you, not even God.

This is not to say that we should not seek counsel from, or collaborate with, others. Those abilities are very necessary for life, too! But, when it comes to knowing what is next on your path for your soul to fulfill its destiny, only you can know that. How could anyone know what is destined for your soul, except for you?

One thing that helps in trusting ourselves is to know the self as a soul, because then it becomes clear that we are moving through life guided by the wisdom of the eternal self. Knowing myself as a spiritual being was the most important piece of knowledge I ever received. By received, I mean "understood through experiencing it." This understanding shifted my perspective from the finite to the infinite. It took me from the instability of an ever-changing world to the unlimited safety of the eternal self ... and it helped me trust myself and my inner knowing infinitely more!

5 *Cheer Yourself On*

Acknowledging our effort and perseverance is vital to our growth and self-worth. We have to be our own cheerleader. There are so many times on the path to learning or mastering something that we fall short of our desired results. Normally, we will not meet our aim, or what we believe is possible, right away. We learn by failing. And it's not how many times we fail that matters; it's how many times we get back up. Eventually, we hit the target (or some variation of the target), as we get shaped by what we've learned along the way.

We need to become a loving parent to the part of our self that is an eternally innocent child. That child who keeps trying to walk, despite having fallen down a thousand times. When we were little, we didn't judge ourselves for falling. Falling gave us the incentive to keep trying. We shrugged off the fall as nothing and kept our eye on the prize. Otherwise, we would not have learned to walk; we would have given up. The fact that we are walking proves that, in the face of a thousand failures, we kept on trying and believing that we would eventually do it.

Our parents or guardians were usually there cheering on our attempts, even though it took so long to accomplish the goal. But then, as many of us got older and became capable of accomplishing things more quickly, we were often subjected to people's expectations for our immediate success. Instead of cheering us on, they told us we were not doing it right if we did not ace new tasks relatively fast. We picked up on those cues of perfectionism and embedded them deep into our subconscious. That's when we became the perfectionistic parent to ourselves.

Failure is a stepping stone to victory, not a character defect. We all know that practice doesn't make us perfect, but it makes us very capable. We can't become good at something worthwhile without having to travel, sometimes with great difficulty, up the learning curve. Old habits die hard, and new ones are hard to form. There cannot be success from the outset. So, that means that every time we fail at something, we have to give ourselves kudos for attempting something new. It takes courage to try our hand at something that we are not proficient at, or to get up after falling.

Always acknowledge your sincere effort and never see yourself as a failure. You are the one person who should never give up on you. You are the only person who can fulfill your destiny and bring your gifts into the world in a vitally important way!

See the wider timeline by zooming out, and do not

get caught up in any one situation, scene, or character flaw. Jump the momentary hurdles and keep moving towards your joy. Do not allow yourself to feel defeated. Failure is simply a way to learn what doesn't work so that we can keep narrowing down what does. Instead of focusing on what is wrong with you, or your life, think about how you can keep moving toward your vitality and fulfillment.

When we love and appreciate our self in this way, we will have the confidence and support from within to keep trying; our enthusiasm will continue to build. We will develop trust in ourselves. We will not belittle, lose hope or lose faith in ourselves, but we will have our own back in this school called life. We will know that we have a very solid supporter in our corner.

If you already have an unconditionally supportive relationship with yourself, good job! That means you can be more unconditional with others, too, since the relationship we have with our self creates the foundation for how we relate to other people. And everyone needs more cheerleaders in their corner. We must cheer ourselves and each other forward, towards the win.

Our tolerance for someone's current weaknesses is equal to the amount of love we have for them. So, if you find you are too hard on yourself vs. supportive, encouraging, and unconditional – love is the answer. Start to love yourself as much as you can, because you deserve it. It's the best investment of love you will ever make.

9

Creating a Relationship of Trust with God

1 *Open To Possibility*

God can be a loaded word (or not), depending on how we have experienced it. As you saw at the beginning of my journey, when I started exploring the existence of God, I didn't even use the word "God." It felt strange to use a word that represented something that may or may not be real. That's why I said, "*Whatever* you are..." I didn't want to convince myself that God was there or get attached to a particular outcome. I wanted the truth, without the influence of hope. Therefore, I kept it very ambiguous in the naming department. If God didn't exist, OK, but what did I have to lose by being open to the possibility of God? The main thing was that I became open, realizing that there are many things I did not know. That left a lot of room for learning and understanding new possibilities.

Over the last fifteen years, I have been fortunate to feel God's love and support in countless ways. This connection is so familiar now that I know immediately when I am in contact with God. In the same way that we receive certain energy from each person around us, God has a very specific energy, too. In my experience, this love gives me a feeling of belonging and is radiant, calm, peaceful, energizing, and stabilizing.

When different people experience God, they refer to him/her in different ways and by different names, e.g., the Divine, Source, Most High, Father, Mother, etc. As you read this section, I invite you to relate to *God* in the way that makes the most sense to you right now. If you are not comfortable with that word, replace it with what you are comfortable with. The name reference isn't important. The experience is what matters. Experiences can expand and open our awareness to things that were not previously in our perceived realm of possibility.

If you already have a relationship with God, there may be aspects of God's unlimited heart that you still have yet to discover. I know that I am always excited to understand God at deeper levels than I already do. Just as our relationships with others are constantly evolving, our relationship with God is also evolving. Is it possible that we have been looking at God through one lens, but that there is so much more to God's unlimited personality than what we have been seeing? Being open can allow this relationship to enter new and uncharted territories, ones in which we may feel closer and more connected to God than ever before.

2 *Speak Your Truth*

There is a saying in Raja Yoga that *God loves an honest heart.* I have experienced this to be 100% true. Honesty in any relationship is closeness-promoting. Those relationships where we can be unfiltered are the ones in which we feel the most supported to be our authentic selves. We want the people in our lives to be real with us, to be able to relax and show their true colors. The same is true for God in my experience. God wants an uncensored relationship with the real you, the whole you.

You may be someone who has a clear connection to, and experience of, God. Or, you may be unsure if God exists. I was unsure about God's existence, hence the middle part of my heart's mantra: "*if* you are..." Not knowing is not an issue. If you do or do not know if God exists; if you do or do not have a relationship with God; if you want to explore having one, or simply want to deepen the one you already have – communicate exactly what you are feeling, unfiltered, heart-to-heart.

Some people believe that God always knows what's in their heart. However, in my experience, God does not meddle in our lives, uninvited. That Eternal One is the best parent who is there to guide and support us; but He does not force anything upon us, not even connection. We have to make an effort to connect with God. Even if that is: "I don't believe in you, I don't know if you are there, but I'm open to seeing if you are." That's a great starting point – being real – which opens up the communication and invites God in. Relationships are a two-way street.

In my experience with God, whenever I share what's in my heart, it is like a magic door of connection. Just think about what it's like with people you care about: when they share something from the heart with you, it allows for a deepening of that connection. So too, in the relationship with God, it is important to be transparent with where you are. The authenticity of speaking your truth melts God's heart and forges a closer connection. Trust me on this one.

3 *Better Listen Up*
_____

If listening to our intuition is *Listening In*, then receiving communication from God is *Listening Up*. God communicates with us in different ways which are sometimes mysterious and new. In my journey, God started responding to me long before I knew it was

God. I was being shown and feeling things that I had not experienced before, which were new forms of subtle communication.

At first, it was like learning a new language: a language which was beyond words. Since then, I have become more sensitive to different kinds of subtle communication; not just with God, but with other people in my life, too. Now I realize that subtle communication is happening all the time.

Regarding the way we each receive subtle communication: Some people are clairaudient (hearing a voice/s), some are clairvoyant (seeing images), some are clairsentient (recognizing feelings), and others are claircognizant (knowing). I mostly receive messages in the latter two forms, although on occasion I have seen and heard things that are forms of communication.

One clear example of this is: One morning, while I was meditating at the meditation center, I got a very clear thought that Vivek and I had to move from where we were living *right away;* and that we must move closer to the meditation center. It was a strong thought that pierced my mind, which was otherwise silent. It definitely felt like a firm and urgent instruction.

After I finished meditating, I began to drive around the block near the meditation center. On the next street, there was a sign for an apartment for rent. I called the number, and the woman told me that it would be available to view later in the week since the wood floor had just been varnished. I went home and told Vivek the strong thought I'd had in meditation and asked if we could go see the apartment. He agreed.

When we first walked into the apartment, we were impressed. Vivek said that, although it was good, it was illogical to move in a rush. He said that we should take our time to look properly for a place, in the summer, after a couple of big events of ours were over. He wanted to compare it with other places and not just jump in.

I still felt strongly that I was being pushed for us to move right away and not wait even a few days, despite it being illogical to move in such a rush! I didn't know why I felt this; I just knew I did. He had not received the strong signal that I did, so it was hard for him to agree to what seemed like a very rash and unnecessary (not to mention stressful) decision. I received this clear instruction in my meditation on Monday, and we saw the apartment on Friday.

On Saturday night, just a few minutes shy of midnight, two people tried to break into our house. We were sitting in the bedroom when we heard the familiar, long creak of the screen door opening. There was no mistaking that sound. We had locked both locks on the screen door, so we knew something was wrong. Our car was parked just outside the door, so they must have known we were home. This prompts one to wonder what their intentions were and made this near-home invasion that much more frightening.

Luckily, we were still awake on a phone call to India with Vivek's sister Monika. After being startled by the spotlights coming on outside and hearing the screen door swing open, we called the police. By the time the police arrived, whoever was trying to break in had fled the scene. The face of the security camera outside our door had been spray-painted, the two locks on our metal security door were broken, the two locks on our inner wooden door were also broken (when we went to grab the handle of the inside door, the entire handle came off in our hands). The only lock that wasn't breached was a tiny little safety lock that went up into the ceiling from inside. Fortunately, we had locked it that night.

After that, Vivek was ready to pack his bags and move, regardless of how inconvenient the timing was! Within a few days, we had moved into the new apartment by the meditation center.

I think that experience convinced Vivek to be more trusting of the divine signals that come; and reaffirmed the importance of listening to them for me, especially when they come while in silent connection with God. This is knowing the importance, protection, and interactive process of *Listening Up*.

Even though God communicates to the soul in subtle ways, those messages can be loud and clear to us once we are tuned in on that level. Many people already know the methods God uses to communicate with them. For me, it is when I go deep into the sweet, silent stillness of meditation that I can feel God's energy and if it's needed, His guidance. Sometimes it's a very clear feeling. Other times, it's like getting taken beyond everything that's happening in life and being shown the bigger picture. The important thing is to make time to connect and listen. It is not a one-way communication.

God can communicate back to us in so many ways; we just have to be open and available to receive the messages. Sometimes this communication reaches us through other people, too. Often, you can recognize it because it's out of the scope of what you normally experience. After hearing the experiences of so many fellow yogis, I know that God communicates with each of us in unique ways that are suited to how we can best be reached. But we must allow ourselves to enter the more subtle space of the soul when we want to connect with God, because the subtle realm of existence is where God is. To receive communication from God, we have to find a way to get on the same frequency – the same channel. For some people, this is prayer. For others, it is meditation. In both cases, we are focusing and channeling our energy toward connecting with the Divine.

Similar to making time for our self (as we did in Chapter 7, EST), we also need EGT: Essential God Time. Ideally, we will eventually be aware of our connection with God *all the time*. But that is something that takes practice and time to develop. Good relationships require the investment of quality time, to grow, and then we see the maturing of them. Therefore, we need to set aside a specific time to be in this unlimited connection, without any other distractions.

This focused time is never time wasted, but is always time saved. I've seen that, after I make time to meditate and connect with God, the clutter of random thoughts leaves my mind and stillness fills it. This peacefulness of mind allows me to work more efficiently after I'm done. By connecting with God's energy, we recalibrate our energy back to its most divine, clear, and powerful level. In God's presence, we are automatically reminded of our purest vibration; a place where we operate from the highest and most benevolent intentions.

4 *Experiment & Explore*

You already know that connecting to God's love and energy through meditation has been a very important part of my journey back to trust. This stabilizing practice takes me from a mundane awareness to a vaster spiritual awareness. For me, meditation is not just relaxation— it is also insightful and refreshing. It allows me to tune into that frequency where I can easily connect with God. Since I have experienced God's energy so many times, that frequency has become deeply familiar to my energetic system. So now, simply remembering the frequency of God's vibration acts as a switching on of that connection.

One of the greatest surprises on this journey has been experiencing the many aspects of God's personality. I've shared some of those moments in my story where I felt God's unfathomable love. And there have been so many other moments, in between those larger experiences, that I have felt God's heart and energy encouraging me in beautiful ways.

In Raja Yoga, they describe God in so many ways, e.g., the Ocean of Love, Ocean of Bliss, Ocean of Peace, the True Guide, Beloved, Mother, Father, Teacher, and Friend. God has an unlimited quantity of all divine qualities. We can experience different aspects of the personality of God in a variety of ways and relationships. Not dissimilarly to how we can relate to others in many different types of relationships, e.g., the same person can be a son, brother, friend, father, beloved, etc. We are unlimited in the types of relationships we can have with others, and with God, it is even more unlimited.

We all connect with God in different ways, so God also relates to us in diverse ways. If you have always thought of God as only the Father, try to connect to God as the Mother. Then see the qualities you experience from God in that relationship. Or try my favorite: God as your Friend. You may be surprised to find new heart-opening ways to connect with God, or discover aspects of God's personality that you hadn't felt before. God will connect with us in the ways that we can, and need to connect. God is unlimited, but we also have to be!

5 *Relax & Enjoy*

We can have humorous, fun, and playful aspects in our relationship with God, too. You may already be experiencing this in your relationship with God, but, in case you're not: Breaking News! This relationship doesn't have to be so serious all the time.

Do things with God that you would do with your best friend: dance, go for a walk, have a cup of tea. You can enjoy God's companionship and connect with His energy, during these everyday moments. Bebe used to sit for an hour in the morning with God and her cup of tea. That was when she would have a sweet, heart-to-heart conversation with God. She would come out of those tea-time meditations with so much light in her eyes.

I have had wonderful playful responses and joyful, light, and funny moments with God, too. One example of those sorts of moments was on a hot summer day that was busy, morning to evening. I was scheduled to teach a meditation class after work. I was craving an ice cream cone, but there was no time between work and class to go and get it, let alone eat it. The class I was teaching that night was about God.

When a student showed up for the class, he had *three* half-gallon boxes of ice cream, one of which was my favorite (mint chocolate chip, which he had no way of knowing). When I opened the door, my jaw dropped open. He told me, "I got a strong thought to stop and bring some ice cream!" Even though this was a small thing, it was a very sweet gesture of communication to me from God; that even my playful desire to have ice cream could be fulfilled. This was not the first time something like this happened. When this happened before, it was also when I wanted to do something for myself, but I put aside my own plan so that I could do something for another. By renouncing my momentary desire and opting to contribute to the wellbeing of someone else, I was taken care of generously (more than I would have been otherwise).

That's not to say that it's God's job to fulfill all our desires. I think it happened because I let go of the desire and did what was pure-hearted at that time. That generosity came back, multi-fold. These experiences have been unique moments when I have learned something through sweet, playful communication. These moments have taught me that, when I do what's right and put the benefit of everyone ahead of myself, I will always be taken care of (even in the smallest ways).

In my experience, God's energy is stable, loving, available, and as specific as it is expansive. But His energy is also playful and fun. Connecting with God takes me into my peace, bliss, and serenity very quickly. It also teaches me not to take everything so seriously. Try making God your companion and playmate. You might just wish you had done it sooner.

10

Creating Relationships of Trust with Others

1 *Not About You*

We have all heard this many times: *Don't take anything personally.* But how do we accomplish that, if we are stuck in the throes of trying to *fix* everything and *be* everything for everyone? I've found that we naturally stop taking things personally once we have realized who we are and have restored our self-worth. When we know our value, we stop seeking approval from others; we become clear about what is (and what isn't) our responsibility. Hint: How others choose to act *isn't*.

There was a time in my life when I took everything personally. The way people felt, how they treated me, how they reacted in situations – even the way they looked at me – was all *my* responsibility! Wow, how powerful I was, that I could have so much influence over them.

What a backward reality to live in!

Many of us have internalized the same false perception of being responsible for other people's feelings and behavior. We usually do this during our impressionable childhood, when our parents or siblings blame us for their anger or for how they choose to react. The way another person perceives, acts, and reacts is *their* responsibility. It can be very easy to make those closest to us the scapegoats for our short tempers or dissatisfactions, but how we choose to react is solely within our power. If someone is the rudest or the nicest to you, that's because of them – not you. We have nothing to do with the way others choose to live or how they choose to treat people.

Not. Even. A. Little. Bit.

Take any challenging situation: For instance, getting into a small fender bender that is partly your fault. The person in the other car could react in countless ways. They could get out and want to fight, taking out their stress from the situation on you. Or they could just as easily get out, calmly assess the situation, and move forward toward a solution (all the time keeping their composure and treating you like a human being). What does either response have to do with you?

Our actions are always our choice, and it's incumbent upon us do the best that we can. Other people's perceptions, actions, and reactions are on them. They may try hard to convince you that you are to blame for the way they are feeling and reacting, but don't fall for that. It's impossible to force someone to feel something.

I don't take anything personally anymore; because I know it's not about me, it's about them. It's comical to me now when someone still believes that someone else is responsible for how they feel and then blames them. When that's projected at me, I sometimes giggle quietly to myself.

How someone acts and reacts, whatever qualities they express or don't express, the extent to which they do or do not take responsibility for their behavior: that has everything to do with them, and nothing to do with you. There is a compelling concept: *People are not against you – they are simply for themselves*. It's not about you.

Once this is deeply ingrained in our system, we are liberated from the self-made prison of trying to fix everything and be everything for others. Knowing what is, and what isn't, our responsibility greatly enhances our ability to have healthy relationships. When we stop trying to fix that which isn't our responsibility (codependency), we can put our energy into how we want to show up for ourselves and others (interdependence). Our time and energy will no longer be wasted.

What IS yours to take personally is truly personal: how you are acting and reacting. As much and as long as we are waiting for someone to come and save us from our problems and suffering, to the same extent we will make others responsible for our feelings and actions. When we take full responsibility for our needs, feelings, actions, and reactions, there is no longer a need to blame anything on anyone else.

2 *Benefit Of Doubt*

Nobody is perfect, so let's accept that. We are lucky to get it right as often as we do. The sooner we accept that no one is perfect, the more we will be real with others and allow them to be real with us. When we accept everyone where they are, we create an environment where evolution and growth are far more likely.

When we know better, we do better. Sometimes we don't have the knowledge or experience yet to do something another way. At other times, we don't have the willpower to implement what we know. Whichever the case, each person is working with what's in their toolbox. Is it not better to see in what ways you can be supportive, and not make someone feel bad about not having all the tools? How is making someone feel bad going to help anyway? A great rule of thumb is to give the benefit of the doubt, and know that everyone is doing their best.

It's important to remember that people are operating out of their current operating system (OS). Perhaps you can see that they could use an update to their OS, and how that would be beneficial for them. You have already made that update and realize that, if they update their OS, it will make their life a lot easier. But it is *their* OS ... and they will only update it when they want to, and after they realize, themselves, that it's time. Until then, they will continue using the OS they are comfortable and familiar with. Realization can only happen when the individual is ready; it cannot happen before or be forced. Sometimes, it only happens when the pain and discomfort of not updating becomes too much.

If we stop holding ourselves as prisoners of expectation, then we stop holding others in the prison of expectations, too. It is unrealistic to think anyone will get it right all the time. Instead of being critical, we should encourage one another's belief in themselves so that they can build the confidence to keep moving towards their highest potential. It's easy to get nitpicky in relationships; and the closer you are, the easier it is.

Nitpicking is pointless! Nobody is here to make you happy, or comfortable, or to grow on your timeline. They are exactly where they need to be, right now, in *their* journey. Do not point out what they are doing wrong. If you want to give suggestions, do it with love. You can share how doing it another way has been beneficial for you, but never expect that they will see it or do it just like you do. Everyone is different.

A great way to give the benefit of the doubt is to see the childlike part in others that always needs encouragement and a safe place to land after they feel they have "messed up." In the same way that we can be our own supportive parent and cheerleader, giving others the benefit of the doubt will give them the support, space, and time to make their needed shifts, too. All the while giving us time to focus on change – where our power lies – within our self.

3 *Give Others Time*

Like EST and EGT, there is GOT. We cannot make others take time for themselves, but we can be mindful of giving others their space and allow them JOMO (the Joy of Missing Out, or the pleasure of taking a break from social activity) whenever they need or want time alone. This is especially true in relationships; and the closer you are, the more it is true.

In relationships, it's easy to get enmeshed with each other. So, we need time to disconnect from others and stabilize within ourselves. When we are with other people, we are co-mingling energetically. We are consciously and unconsciously picking up their energy and signals; i.e., when we are with others, we're in the "on" position. And, we all need time in the "off" position. It wears anything out to be "on" all the time!

So, the more you love and care for someone, the more you must make sure that they have as much space as they need. Taking space is good self-care, and giving space is a great way to care for each other. Most of the time, when we are in relationships with others, we are in their orbit in some way; but it doesn't have to be *closely* at every moment. If we are not allowing others in our lives essential alone time, then we are suffocating ourselves, them, and the relationship. Like a fire, if it doesn't have air, it cannot grow.

This time alone, this time apart, serves the valuable

function of allowing us to become more self-aware and self-sufficient. It also allows us to tune in to what is next for us. We each have to know how much EST we need, and how much we need to GOT. Remember: *Absence makes the heart grow fonder.* So, take some space and give some space ... it's good for everyone.

4 *In Your Lane*

As individual actors in this unlimited play of existence, we can only know what's in our own script and coming up next in our own part. To create great relationships, we need to play our part in the drama of life to the best of our ability. And we must trust that others are doing the same. We will not be able to play our part well if we are consumed by worrying about how the other actors will play their parts. This is where we must check ourselves before we wreck ourselves: by keeping our focus where we have the power to make the greatest contribution to the play.

In other words, we each have our way of journeying through life. We only know our thoughts, feelings, and motives; and our past, present, and future potential. We do not know the thoughts, feelings, past, present, and future potential of others. We can guess, but we will never have the complete picture. Therefore, we cannot assume that we know what someone else is capable of or should do with their life. There is a saying: *It's asinine to assume*. How can we possibly know what others should do, when they are being guided by their own heart and soul?

Why is it so hard to trust that others know best how to play their parts? Why do we ever think that we know what they should do? When we feel out of control in our own life – or fear losing our perceived control – we resort to trying to control others and the environment around us. If we find ourselves trying to direct or control others, we need to search where, in our own life, we need to feel more safe and secure. Once we are purposely moving forward in our own life, then we will no longer try to dictate what others do. We will have respect for each individual's journey.

A sign of becoming more secure in yourself is a decrease in assumption, judgment, and the need to control. The judgment of others is never productive. It keeps the one who is judging in a self-created prison; coloring their energy with the same negativity that they are assuming about the other person. When we judge, we become the ones who suffer because we are operating out of ego and fear. The result of actions done out of ego and fear is always a loss to the self. We end up creating more lack and loss because of the underlying selfish vibrations we are putting out.

In each lifetime, we are all here to accomplish specific things and learn particular lessons. We all go through ups and downs. Not only can we not know what others need to do, but we cannot stop others from experiencing the things they need to along their soul's journey – even if there are difficult situations that have to be faced. As individuals, our karma comes back to us, as feedback, to help us course-correct. Our difficulties can become our greatest teachers in this way.

We also have to be careful not to try to make others in the image we desire for them, in order to make ourselves more comfortable. Many of us have the habit of trying to make our own life easier by pointing out what we do not like in others. We hope that our prodding will change them. Allow people to be exactly who they are. Don't assume that they are trying to make your life difficult, or that they are there to make you feel safe or better about yourself. That is *your* job! Trusting the journeys of others is the best thing we can do for ourselves and for them.

5 *Healing With Others*

We are not on this journey alone. We are traveling through life, space, and time together: with our families, friends, colleagues, etc. Life is dependent on being connected and taking care of each other. Just as much as we need to be self-sufficient and self-sovereign, having our self-respect and autonomy, we also need to feel safe and close with those around us. Love and care are essential; not just to survive, but to thrive. When we can trust the love that we have with ourselves, God, and others – we feel embraced and supported from within, above, and without. Then the heart feels safe enough to open up and fill up.

One of the most important lessons I have learned through Vivek's work in Heart IQ is that our greatest emotional pain has come through our interactions with others; and so our greatest emotional healing has to come from there, too. The emotional wounds and pain that have been created in this lifetime can leave energetic imprints on the soul. We carry unhealed energetic imprints within ourselves, creating blocks in our energy, doubt in our capacity, and fear around connecting with others.

When we have blockages in relating to others; when we cannot get close, and we shut down; or when we have unhealthy behavior patterns in relationships, we cannot simply meditate, read, or talk them away. We have to work on those things from the root energetic causes, the seeds from where they started. We must replace those energetic imprints of fear and unsafety with the imprints of trust, safety, and support. In other words, we have to rewire those parts of our subtle and physical nervous systems.

That's why the four points mentioned previously in this chapter, about creating healthier and more trusting relationships with others (e.g. not taking anything personally, giving the benefit of the doubt, giving others space and time, and staying in our lane by not trying to control others or the environment) are easy to understand, but quite hard to implement.

When dealing with our self and God, there can be hang-ups and hurdles to overcome within ourselves. However, when we try to open our hearts and trust others, there are usually walls galore that we have built up to protect ourselves. After having been hurt, abandoned, or shut down in our lives by the people we have trusted the most, it becomes almost impossible to fully put the above suggestions into practice – even when we want to. We have to knock down the walls, with love!

It's incredible how fast we can progress in the area of forming deeply trusting relationships with others when we allow ourselves to become *real and vulnerable together*. The healing of our trust in relationships with others is something we cannot do by ourselves. We are each other's mirrors and, because of that, each other's healers.

That type of emotional healing, where the nervous system is rewired, so that deeply trusting relationships are possible again, is a hands-on process. It is a feeling and healing process (not a thinking process), which happens in a safe space, created by someone who knows how to guide us in opening the parts of our heart that have been shut down. This approach can be a faster route to healing than traditional therapy. In talk therapy, people can get stuck in their story – trying to resolve emotional blockages by figuring them out intellectually – without actually accessing their blockages at the emotional or energetic levels.

I gained so much, so quickly, participating in heart-centered coaching, heart circles, and retreats. Taking the time to heal with others the places where we have been wounded (both knowingly and unknowingly), is the fast-track, holistic way to develop more trust in our relationships. Some of the great coaches that have guided Vivek's and my journey in this are Christian Pankhurst and Tej Steiner. The type of heart-opening work that they teach is so effective that we combine it, along with other healing modalities, in all our retreats and coaching.

Remember: When it comes to changing how we interact with others, reopening the heart is not a process that we do from the head. The head can understand, but we must feel into our hearts to heal at the energetic and emotional levels. Only in this way can we piece back together our hearts, when they have been broken in relationships with others in the past.

11

Creating a Relationship of Trust with Matter

1 *Appreciating Your Vehicle*

So far, I have shared some things that I learned in my journey to creating more supportive and trusting relationships with the self, God, and others. Those are the connections with*in* ourselves, *up* to the Divine, and *out* towards others which deal with our relationships to conscious beings. But, we also have another vital relationship: our relationship with matter. Matter is what literally allows us to be *down* to earth. It enables us to enjoy the wonder of ourselves and the universe on a multi-sensory level.

The relationship between consciousness and matter is a constant, energetic give-and-take encompassing all tiers of being: spiritual, mental, emotional, energetic, and physical. Meaning: the thoughts and feelings that we souls have, energetically and physically affect matter, and vice versa. Awareness of the subtleties of this symbiotic relationship is essential if we want to maximize the potential of our time here on earth.

Our relationship with matter encompasses everything made up of the elements and especially includes the matter which is the closest to us. As our faithful companions, our bodies are our vehicles of matter which help us get from the starting point of our lives to the end. They work tirelessly so that we can squeeze as many juicy moments out of life as possible! Each day they perform millions of minute functions, keeping us alive. For example, a single neuron in the body can send as many as a thousand nerve impulses in one second. The human body is the most complex machine in the world, with trillions of working parts. And these machines are self-cleaning and self-healing. What an invention of nature, that we are so fortunate to have the use of!

Our bodies give us immense pleasure by enabling us to experience unlimited sensory wonders. Our eyes, ears, nose, mouth, and sense of touch enable us to interact with the world in a plethora of spellbinding ways. How often do we think of our bodies in this way? Do we look at them with amazement? If your answer is "yes," then keep being awesome.

Sometimes, instead of appreciating our bodies, we use our time over-focusing on how they *look*. Modern society would have us believe that our body's purpose is to be a window display for the non-existent Store of

Perfection. I learned in my twenties that ruminating over my appearance was a monumental waste of time. Was my nose too big? What about my feet? Was there too *much* fat or too *little* fat, depending on the location? Does it really matter? The health and functionality of our body is what's important. Our appearance does not give us value; *how we value ourselves* does.

The purpose of our eyes is to see and connect with the beauty in our world; not to be a certain color. The purpose of our nose is to breathe fresh air and smell the flowers; not to be a certain size or shape. The purpose of our lips are to speak sweet words and eat delicious food; not to have a certain amount of volume to them. The list goes on and on. *Look at how much our bodies do for us every day,* and then examine how we look at them with dislike or get nitpicky about small external details. Imagine if you were on the receiving end of that unfair behavior: after a hard day's work, making full effort to do a *million* tasks, to keep everything operating smoothly in such a sophisticated machine, your boss looks at you disapprovingly because of *one* insignificant thing.

Physical beauty standards constantly change, which means some features will be considered beautiful at a particular time and not at another. Our bodies age and change, and that's a natural part of life. If we spend our time on this planet trying to fit a societally-determined beauty standard, our precious time will be wasted. That's time, which can be used to create, enjoy life, and express our gifts (which is what our bodies are here to allow us to do).

Nobody is perfect by any beauty standard, but our bodies *are* perfect for us. It is our custom car, designed only for us. Treat it like a Tesla: the most technologically advanced, energy-efficient, and sophisticated piece of machinery you have ever owned.

We need to change the relationship we have with our bodies from one of complaints and corrections, to one of gratitude and wonder. Try beginning each day by appreciating your body. When you wake up, give it some love; let it know that it's doing a great job. Thank it! Positive reinforcement is so important in this relationship with our bodies. Matter responds to consciousness and follows a benevolent path when given the right energy! Giving it love and appreciation creates an environment where it can thrive. When we have gratitude for the matter that we are so inseparably connected to, a healthy relationship cannot help but blossom.

2 *Listening For Signals*

Not only do we communicate with our bodies through our thoughts and feelings, but our bodies constantly talk to us, too. In fact, our bodies converse with us all the time. They let us know when they need to be recharged, when they need fuel, and what kind of fuel they run best on. They also let us know when they need movement and stretching.

Through a variety of signals, the body talks to us. If it is being affected negatively, it creates symptoms or pain to let us know; and it can even tell us the solution sometimes. One example of this is when I had a fungal infection on one of my nails. The infection wasn't going away with natural remedies, over the counter products, or prescribed creams. Out of nowhere, I began to crave cinnamon. It was a strong signal, so I listened. I started adding cinnamon to as many foods as I could. Within a couple of weeks, the fungus was gone and never came back. I realized that my body communicated the cure.

Realizing that our body is regularly communicating with us makes us more apt to listen and better respond to its needs. When we listen and respond to its suggestions, we will be in better health and alignment. When waking up or before sleeping, after giving some love and appreciation to your trusty vehicle, take a few minutes to listen in and see if it needs anything from you. Maybe it needs to stretch, a little massage, or plenty of water. You may be surprised how much it communicates and guides you.

3 *Big Game Changer*

Everything in nature comes with a natural operating system and, when allowed to go through its processes unhampered, works efficiently and provides generously. We only have to cooperate by living *knowledgeably*, in harmony and balance, with regard for our bodies, all sentient beings and the planet. Right now, the innumerable systemic diseases in our bodies and nature reveal that we are out of alignment with what is natural and harmonious. The great need of this time is for us to live in a conscious, compassionate, balanced, and benevolent way on the earth and within our bodies. We can start this process by understanding how we affect our bodies and the planet through our individual choices. Then, after understanding our impact, we can resolve to increase the level of *regard* and *care* with which we treat our bodies, other sentient beings, and the planet.

In my early twenties, I decided to experiment with becoming a vegetarian (and then a vegan) for health reasons. After I switched my diet, my skin cleared up, immunity increased, and I had more energy. My body seemed to function better in every way. I noticed more clarity of mind and calmness in my energy. It was clear to me that I was functioning (and vibrating) at a higher level on a whole-food, plant-based diet. I was creating a cycle of health by inputting pure vibrational food in my system and experiencing more vitality as a result.

Contrarily by eating animals and animal byproducts, I was sustaining a cycle of suffering.

Animals are harmed when they are separated from their parents at birth, throughout their confined lives, and at their unnatural deaths. As conscious beings, the pain and fear they feel gets stored in their bodies. Then when people eat animals and their byproducts, they are also eating the energy of sorrow that is created and stored in their bodies. Both sides are suffering a lot from this unnatural arrangement. Since animal products are not meant for the human body, we get heart disease, cancer, stroke, diabetes, obesity, and many other illnesses (see *The China Study* for compelling research on this, which was conducted over a long period of time and shows how animal product consumption creates a plethora of modern health issues).

Moving away from an animal-based diet is the single biggest, game-changing decision that we can make as individuals for the health of ourselves and the planet. If you haven't done your research, please do. There is no reason that animals, people, or the planet should suffer unnecessarily. The earth has given us a vast array of colorful and delicious foods to eat. Our bodies are naturally suited to be vegetarian, which is evident by the digestive system we have. That's why we feel so much better when we switch to a balanced vegetarian diet because eating that way is in alignment with our internal (and external) ecosystem.

Another part of this cycle of sorrow is that livestock produces methane gas which warms the globe twenty times faster than carbon dioxide. This means that animal farming is a mammoth driver of climate change. The only way to change the output of this equation is to change the input. Our health, animal welfare, and the planet's health are intimately intertwined. If you don't feel motivated to change your diet for yourself, consider doing it for your children, the animals, and the planet. At least start by learning the facts, so you can make an informed choice.

I have yet to meet someone who switched to a balanced vegetarian diet, whose health was not greatly improved after making the switch. And, thanks to modern technology, we have healthy replacement options for all of the animal products that we have become accustomed to. These plant-based options are becoming more and more delicious and harder to differentiate from the "real thing." Using those replacements can help make the transition to healthier choices easier.

I understand that it's not easy to change habits that we have had since childhood – and that there are often deeper factors that influence how we eat, and why. I really respect when someone makes this change, even though it may not be easy. That's why, in my holistic coaching practice, I feel passionate about guiding clients through the life-changing process of adopting an energizing whole food, plant-based diet. When they follow everything we've discussed, after a couple of weeks, they begin to glow. There is an obvious, night-and-day difference once they elevate their relationship with their body and food.

They have less brain fog, an increase in energy, clearer skin, more pleasure in cooking and eating, enhanced connection to their body and its signals, weight reduction and the ability to maintain it, more strength and stamina while running and exercising, and more. *It is not magic,* but our bodies run better on the fuel that is meant for them! If we water our plants with soda, do you think they will live very well or for very long?

We have to get back to what's natural for our bodies in order to promote our health and care for our planet. There is no time like the present to take care of nature and our bodies with focused dedication and an unstoppable fire of spirit. The path of least resistance may be the most comfortable, but that is not what will create the most energy, health, vitality, and joy.

4 *Consumer To Contributor*

In my experience of cycling through several periods of accumulation and decluttering, I have noticed that the more I accumulate, the less free I feel. We usually need far less than we are taught to believe. Happiness, love, belonging, time, knowledge, expression, and experience cannot be bought. The *most important things* are free, and the most important thing is *to be free.* The fewer extra things we have to look after, the more available we are to invest in activities that en*rich* our lives. In today's society, we can easily become hostages of the stuff that we over-accumulate. We are told that if we just have this thing or that thing, we will be happy...

But the truth is, the times in my life where I managed to simplify my material entrapments the most were the most joyful, lush, and productive times in my life. As soon as material things start to dictate my time, I realize it's time to simplify. Simplicity is a big secret to greater freedom. Less is more: less mess, less stress. You free yourself through the practice of simplicity. Check out Mari Kondo; she's got this thing figured out, and she's so sweet in her approach, too.

Think of some of the most brilliant minds of our time, like Warren Buffet or Bill Gates; they keep things simple in their lives, which gives them ample time to focus on creating and giving back. They don't waste: time, energy, or resources. Simplicity is a sign of intelligence, which enables us to hone in on what matters most and not waste time on unnecessary things.

Instead of a consumer-based society, we need a million other types of societies, e.g., a contributor-based society, an experience-based society, a collaboration-based society, a creativity-based society, a generosity-based society, and a love-based society – because only a society operating from such values will be sustainable.

5 *Our Choices Matter*

When we are aware of the pivotal role any relationship plays in our lives, we make an effort to create, nurture, and sustain it. Our relationship with matter is in need of some serious TLC (tender loving care). Nature has an incredible healing capacity which, if supported by our collective compassionate choices, can save what appears to be a sinking ship in a rising ocean. As one of the most intelligent species on the earth, human beings have the power to make conscious choices for the benefit of all. It's our responsibility to reframe this relationship, rededicate ourselves to caring, and remember how fortunate we are to be experiencing life on this gorgeous planet.

Let's be honest: we all like convenience because we have busy lives. Sometimes the last thing we want to do is add anything to our already long to-do list. We are just trying to get through life as simply as possible (in what can be a very complicated world). However, the trade-off is that we are sacrificing long-term sustainability and health for momentary leisure and convenience.

What legacy do we want to leave our children and our children's children? What condition have we created for today's children? Don't they deserve to experience the wonders of nature and good health? Isn't it worth our extra attention and effort? Whose problem is it, anyway? In the reframing of our relationship with our precious planet, every one of us matters.

Understanding that we are conscious beings that impact matter profoundly means that we must focus on learning how to use everything in a way that is in harmony with our planet's ecosystem. Our relationship with matter can be compared to the relationship between a mother and child. Life is nonexistent without a mother; and after the children are older, the care of the mother is the responsibility of the children (to whom she gave life). We gotta take care of Ma!

If we are to support this planet to be in its optimum reality of vitality, then the beings impacting it the most must make conscious choices all the time. Not sometimes. All the time. Along with the wealth of knowledge that we have through *science,* and the wisdom of the soul found in *silence,* we have every opportunity to know our options and make consciously higher choices. We have the technology and information available to first consider our impact, and then make choices based on their viability. But the question is: Are we ready to sacrifice a little convenience to live in a way that ultimately improves our health, quality of life, and long term survival? It's on us, the beings with the most awareness and the highest capacity to affect what happens next on this planet.

Everything is the way it is, either because of our awareness, or lack of awareness. When we take personal responsibility for waking up and coming together to find solutions, everything will begin to shift; and the scales will tilt fully back in the direction of wholesome balance. Our existence depends on each of us showing up with as much love, peace, truth, respect, selflessness, and inclusivity as we can. Then we will be able to squeeze every little bit of joy out of each moment and create a world of trust and harmony together.

It is our duty. If we love ourselves and life, it is our responsibility to vitalize ourselves and the planet with each choice we make and every thought we have. We are the ones who have the power to create or destroy something. We don't want to file *Chapter 11* because we have overspent our resources collectively. Our choices matter, and must be knowledgeable ones; because the only actual convenient thing to do is to live sustainably.

12

Creating a Relationship of Trust with Life

1 *Be Here Now*

As a result of realizing myself as an eternal being, all fear of death was gradually removed. The wider perspective of myself freed me from a sense of being linearly time-bound. I can see and feel the connection between the past and future, as they fuse to create my story; but I also know my power to create, feel, be, and enjoy is only available in the present.

Since the present is surrounded so intimately by the past and future, they can both seep into my awareness from time to time, distracting me from the joy of the current moment. But I now know the importance of pulling my awareness back to where my power lies. I cannot change the past, and the future is dependent on what I do now. This makes it sensible to focus my energy on being in the here and now. In the present, we have the opportunity to squeeze all the juiciness out of life. The more we savor the present moment, the more we enjoy the deliciousness of life.

Being present makes it possible to feel what needs to unfold and flow through us. Then there are no feelings of backlog, regret, or missed opportunities created. It allows us to give our best to every day, one second at a time.

Life is a never-ending journey. We may have a current destination and a plan for how we want to get there; perhaps we have even been there before. However, on a long journey, there are stops, scenery, detours, and traffic in between. We can only see the road just in front of us and must travel a certain distance on it to see the next turn. The optimal way to reach where we are going is to stay present, enjoy the journey, and keep moving forward – one delightful step at a time.

Then, once we reach the destination, there will be a new journey that starts. Therefore, life is not about *a* destination; the destination is to be fully present! In that sense, there is no past and no future ... there is only now.

2 *Cycle Of Generosity*

We never lose when giving, we always win! Whatever we share, energetically always comes back. Newton's 3rd law, which is the scientific version of the law of karma, states that *for every action, there is an equal and opposite reaction.* In my experience, this is the most important natural law governing the universe, to understand. Because, when we deeply understand the law of cause and effect, it enables us to create life consciously. We are the creators of our lives, both in the short and long term. It's just a matter if we are doing it consciously and optimally.

Over the last decade and a half, I have become increasingly aware of how the law of karma works in my life. Raja Yoga taught me that this law is much deeper than just physical actions. Our thoughts, feelings, motivation, and intentions all count as the energy we are dispersing into the universe. And this energy always comes back to us! It's not only important to do good things, but it's even more important to be good-hearted.

Hence, if we continue to live with a pure heart and pure intention, we will always be well taken care of. We only have to focus on what we are sending out. When we use our existence to support, uplift, care, and share, we are adding goodness into the world – and also into our own orbit.

Staying in this natural cycle of benevolence means

that I focus on giving, and do not have to think about receiving. Bestowing is our natural nature. If I constantly follow my instinct to find positive ways to contribute, I will find that I am in a steady stream of generosity, which comes back to support me in unlimited positive ways. Therefore, I do not have to hold back, out of fear of lack.

We can focus our energy on contributing from a place of an open and full heart, without the worry of depletion, because it always returns anyway. This is always true, unless we are giving something we don't have to give, or we expect and need it to come back. Wanting it to come back changes the motivation from one of generosity to one of neediness. In that case, we are putting the energy of lack out into the world, and that's what will come back. That's why it becomes important to understand the subtleties of the law of karma. The more we understand it, the more it empowers us, to be the master creators of our lives.

We don't have to wait for a particular situation to arise so that we can be generous. At every moment, wherever we are, we can add value. Even if we are simply sending good thoughts to someone or spreading pure feelings into the atmosphere, we can add positive energy to the world at any time. And the best news of all is that simply contributing good vibrations to the world can, in itself, give us great joy (because they come back).

The more we give, the happier we feel. When we are in a place of abundance, we can overflow to everyone around us with good energy. That's why it's important to be full of it (good energy)! That means that the requirement for living a life in the cycle of generosity is to have practices that fill you from within; finding that which enables you to take the greatest care of yourself and also affords you a stockpile of love, peace, and happiness from which you can share. Do you know how they say: "you need money to make money?" Well, here we need a wealth of happiness so that we can create an abundance of happiness. We need a wealth of peace to experience an abundance of peace.

When you understand this universal law of energy, you find ways that you can provide the most benefit to all people, places, and situations. You will never lose when you give in this way. You will be unknowingly creating much good and happiness; not only in the present but also for the future. In the cycle of generosity, everything comes naturally when you need it. So there is no need to worry about having enough! Imagine all of us living from our natural state of benevolence; it would be a world of abundance, where everyone is well taken care of.

Note: We cannot look at the law of karma from just one angle ... we need to discern what is benevolent depending on the situation. If we give begrudgingly; or we are in a situation where we are being used, abused or forced to give something when we don't want to, then it is often necessary to remove ourselves from those circumstances. In that type of situation, we are creating more negative karma by disrespecting ourselves, and by reinforcing bad habits in others. The onus is on us to understand the law of karma more deeply so that we can see how it is subtly creating our life. We can then know what will be the most benevolent action in each situation.

3 *Light = Right = Might*

Making choices that are beneficial for ourselves and others impacts our life profoundly. Doing what is right strengthens our self-respect and worthiness, which in turn encourages us to make good decisions. Some may ask, "who determines what is right?" That's where the aspect of light comes in, which here refers to *awareness* and *knowledge*. Light is having access to your inner knowing, awareness, or knowledge of what is the best action for you to take at any moment. So, if we have the Light (awareness/knowledge) of what is Right (the best action), then the result we get is Might (empowerment) from those actions.

We have seen this in action in our lives: When we do something we know to be right for us, it empowers us. And when we don't do what we know to be right for us, it disempowers us. Acting on what we know is the best decision makes us feel good about ourselves, but our conscience bites us when we do something against what we know is right. This can be in the smallest things, not just big ones. For example, you have the thought to smile or interact with someone; but, out of fear or doubt in yourself, you don't. You shy away. Then your conscience bites. Your conscience will bite because you were guided to interact. But, instead of being able to act on your inner knowing, fear, or doubt, decided your actions for you. Then you will feel frustrated that you weren't comfortable enough, to be fully authentic. Instead of empowering you, this creates doubt in your ability to follow your inner wisdom.

That's why it's important to keep working toward always listening to our inner knowing because it either builds up or breaks down our self-worth and trust in ourselves. When we act on what we know is right, we create a deep trust in our ability to do the right thing. If we keep doing that which we know is not good for us – or if we do not rise to meet our greatness – then slowly, over time, we lose trust in our ability to do what is best for us, or anyone else.

To increase our self-worth and keep it intact, we must always act on the wisdom within us. Even if we cannot accomplish it right away, e.g., if we have a habit which we have been trying to stop for thirty years, one which we know is not good for us, but we cannot get it under control yet. In a situation like that, the important thing is to keep working *diligently* towards what our inner guidance is telling us to do. If we listen to the wisdom within us, which is telling us how to course-correct, we will be reinforcing our self-worth; because we are essentially telling ourselves that we are worth the effort. Even if it takes us time, we are still honoring our truth – and empowering ourselves in the process.

Everything in life is made of energy; it's an energy game. Both matter and consciousness are energetic. Energy cannot be created or destroyed, but is always transformed over time. As conscious beings, we have the ultimate opportunity to play this energy game at many different levels, and win; if we know the rules and how to use the tools. One of the rules is: as we make good choices, we get more power. And vice versa. If we make choices that are not good, we lose power. It is time to understand, observe, and play this energy game with full awareness and engagement. By doing so, we can win it; not just for ourselves, but for everyone.

Cultivating everything – from feelings to actions – with the cleanest energy, purest motivation, and highest intentions makes us powerful. Truth in our actions becomes the basis for our power, and our power is the basis for fulfilling our potential.

4 Find Your Practices

Finding practices that improve your quality of life, upgrade your abilities, raise your vibrations, and make your life straight-up better, is critical. For me, the practices of Raja Yoga meditation, silence, and introspection increase my quality of life by bringing clarity, depth of understanding, and refinement to my way of operating in the world.

These practices have helped me expand my knowledge of how life works. They have taught me how to live life in a truly sensible way. For example,. I understand deeply now that life is made up of diametrical pairs which, when in balance, create perfect harmony. Even our natural world operates on the basis of keeping opposites in balance: night and day, winter and summer, birth and death.

When we are in balance, we give importance to both sides of a complementary pair; realizing that for one to be at its best, it must be in harmony with its opposite. For example, each one of these supports and balances the other out: activity and rest, creativity and silence, masculinity and femininity, love and law, flexibility and structure, humility and assertiveness, effort and surrender.

I have seen that when there is balance, vitality is possible. Problems, diseases, and discomfort develop as a result of being out of balance. Finding balance in each area of our life enables us to go from surviving in the throes of ups and downs to thriving on more stable ground. Meditation has enabled me to be tuned in and more aware of when I am in, or out, of balance in the different areas of my life.

One way to notice if you're out of balance: When you feel frustration or discomfort, examine where it's coming from. Once you pinpoint it, you can focus on increasing the harmonizing aspect to balance it out. For example, if you become aware that sitting is causing discomfort in your body, then you need to move. Or, if you become aware that being controlling is affecting your relationships, then work towards letting go while cultivating trust and flexibility.

Besides helping me create more balance in my life, another example of how my meditation has upgraded my quality of life is by making organization easier. As my mind became more silent and still, I noticed that my thoughts, activities, and surroundings became naturally ordered. With less clutter in my mind, it became easier to see what needed to be done and how to accomplish it more efficiently. Since then, my level of organization has been an indication of how clear or cluttered my mind and energy are. I know they are very connected.

Now I have as much love for systems and organization as I do for spontaneity and flow (they balance each other out)! Systems and organization enable us to simplify by not having to think about how to do something each time. In other words, once we have systems and organization in place, we can forget about the little things and focus on the more important things. Systems, organization, and automation can save us a lot of time.

And these are not only systems we devise with our mind. Our intuition and wisdom guide us in how to order things in an effective way that can save us valuable time and energy. I find that my greatest productivity happens when my inner knowing is guiding my mind, and not when my mind is guiding me. The mind can only go on what it has seen before, whereas our inner knowing is innovative. Find what works for you. You will know that you are working in an orderly way when it is done right and saves your time. When our mind is clear, and emotions are calm, we get the right thoughts at the right time.

Meditation is the way that I find clarity and tap into the best and most effective way to accomplish things. Find those practices that continually improve *your* quality of life and help you reach your full potential.

5 *All Together Now*

Just as it's important to find practices that upgrade and support us, it's also important to find company that does the same. Surrounding yourself with people that support your growth is essential, in order to keep moving forward, increase trust, and achieve success in life. They say that we are the equivalent of the five people with whom we keep the most company. I don't think that's literally true, but we *are* influenced by our company – and it colors us tremendously!

A good rule of thumb is to surround yourself with people that you adore, admire, and aspire to become like. They should have so many good qualities that you want to absorb because, by being around them, you will pick up some of their energy and virtues.

We cannot afford to stop moving in the direction of our highest potential, as individuals and collectively. Our lives and world depend on it! Keeping good company is essential for moving forward in life. Good company enables us to share our joy in good times, and uplifts us in difficult times. We are here to cheer each other on!

For every obstacle, there is a solution. Nothing is permanent. Sometimes we have to stop disillusionment and tiredness from convincing us that a problem is permanent. Problems come and go. Sometimes they take longer to go, but they always do go. We are resilient, inventive, and powerful beings. We only need to resolve to keep moving forward, no matter what. And don't be afraid to ask for support when you need it! Because we are all in this together.

Global renewal can only happen through self-renewal, and self-renewal happens by us helping each other. We are all connected and a part of each other's healing. When one of us heals, it affects the whole – and vice versa. We belong to life; we belong to each other. Nothing can change unless we change, *together*.

Now is the time!

Conclusion

So, that's my story. And, as you can see, realizing the truth of my identity as a soul in an eternal, never-ending, swirling dance throughout time changed my life in *every* possible way. Of course, I'm still a work in progress. Out of all the subsequent things I learned to embody and embrace along the way, the biggest thing I have learned is that there is always something more to learn.

Reality is actually wonder-striking good when we open ourselves up to feel and know it as it is; without any filters of limitation. When we cannot see the wonder that life is anymore – when we've become tired, jaded, or just don't know where to start – there is help available to show us how to recalibrate our compass and learn how to trust our inner direction again. There are sources of support that can help us discover just how extraordinary life is.

There is only one prerequisite: Be open. Often, that entails surrendering what we think we know to see if there are things we don't. It's opening our minds and hearts to see what new gems of understanding we might find in the treasure hunt of life. You may find, as I did, that life is much more marvelous than you had previously imagined.

Sometimes, we live in a world too narrow; one constructed by ideas we've been taught to believe, or based on only one side of an experience. But what if there are so many more possibilities available to us, if we can open up ourselves to new adventures and opportunities? Aren't we curious to find out?

I can say from experience that many beautiful opportunities are available if we just ask. Life wants to work *with* us. Powerful co-creation is waiting to take shape *through us* and simply needs enough silent space and self-belief to emerge. It requires that we acknowledge how vital each of our roles is in this cosmic play. We are divine beings, and our power to rebirth a naturally balanced and harmonious world depends upon us recognizing that.

Everything in life is working beneficially behind the scenes to support us. Even the challenges can act as giant wake-up calls, and lead us back to our true north. The darkest moments can become the greatest blessings in disguise, as they did for me.

To trust in ourselves and life fully is to become free. Then we can focus on the joy of being and the joy of being together.

Every Ending is another Beginning

If you would like to stay in touch or learn more about the work that Vivek and I do with our facilitation partner, Yolanda Beckers, please feel free to contact us through our websites.

For Businesses:
www.incompasseffect.com

For Personal Development:
www.mypresentheart.com

Book Website:
www.feduptowonderstruck.com

Resources for the journey, which I have found the most transformative:

Raja Yoga Meditation:
www.brahmakumaris.org

Christian Pankhurst & Heart IQ:
www.heartiq.org

Tej Steiner & Heart Circles:
www.heartcircle.com

Find your heart's mantra
Listen for the signs
Start your practice
Enjoy the life led by your heart and intuition
Of course, don't stop using your head
Sum up the situation and look before you leap
A spiritual journey is led by higher wisdom
Not social opinion nor by fear
It is Love for Truth

Godmother and Aunt Roseanne with Author (age 11)

About the Author

Kristina Kashyap is a lover of life, truth, and authentic heart connections. Her unquenchable thirst for knowledge, paired with her adventurous spirit, has led her to seek the secrets of the universe through direct experiences.

Kristina has been studying spirituality and practicing Raja Yoga meditation for the last sixteen years. She loves to share what has been the most eye-opening and liberating for her on the path of self-discovery. Through her down to earth approach, she makes spirituality, self-love, and self-empowerment easily accessible.

Kristina also has a passion for cultivating health, vitality, and wellness. She is a Holistic Health Coach, and a practitioner of Polarity Therapy, Elemental Reflexology, and Reiki. Knowing the importance of nurturing the self on all levels (spiritually, energetically, emotionally, mentally, and physically), she helps to connect the dots of healing for her clients. She teaches them how to develop more supportive relationships with themselves and others, based on awareness, trust, respect, balance, and love.

Kristina co-facilitates retreats and workshops that nurture the heart, mind, body, and soul, with Vivek Kashyap and Yolanda Beckers, through their companies My Present Heart and Incompass Effect.

Realizations and Notes for the Self